C++ Software Interoperability for Windows Programmers

Connecting to C#, R, and Python Clients

Adam Gladstone

C++ Software Interoperability for Windows Programmers: Connecting to C#, R, and Python Clients

Adam Gladstone
Madrid, Spain

ISBN-13 (pbk): 978-1-4842-7965-6   ISBN-13 (electronic): 978-1-4842-7966-3
https://doi.org/10.1007/978-1-4842-7966-3

Managing Director, Apress Media LLC: Welmoed Spahr
Acquisitions Editor: Jonathan Gennick
Development Editor: Laura Berendson
Coordinating Editor: Jill Balzano

Cover designed by eStudioCalamar

Cover image designed by Freepik (www.freepik.com)

Distributed to the book trade worldwide by Springer Science+Business Media New York, 1 New York Plaza, Suite 4600, New York, NY 10004-1562, USA. Phone 1-800-SPRINGER, fax (201) 348-4505, e-mail orders-ny@springer-sbm.com, or visit www.springeronline.com. Apress Media, LLC is a California LLC and the sole member (owner) is Springer Science + Business Media Finance Inc (SSBM Finance Inc). SSBM Finance Inc is a Delaware corporation.

For information on translations, please e-mail booktranslations@springernature.com; for reprint, paperback, or audio rights, please e-mail bookpermissions@springernature.com.

Apress titles may be purchased in bulk for academic, corporate, or promotional use. eBook versions and licenses are also available for most titles. For more information, reference our Print and eBook Bulk Sales web page at http://www.apress.com/bulk-sales.

Any source code or other supplementary material referenced by the author in this book is available to readers on GitHub via the book's product page, located at www.apress.com/978-1-4842-7965-6. For more detailed information, please visit http://www.apress.com/source-code.

Printed on acid-free paper

Table of Contents

About the Author

Adam Gladstone is a software developer. He has over 20 years of experience in investment banking, building software mostly in C++ and C#. For the last few years, he has been developing data science and machine learning skills, particularly in Python and R after completing a degree in maths and statistics. He currently works at Virtu Financial Inc. in Madrid as an Analyst Programmer. In his free time, he develops tools for natural language processing.

About the Technical Reviewer

Ockert J. du Preez is a passionate coder and always willing to learn. He has written hundrcds of developer articles over the years detailing his programming quests and adventures. Recently, he has written the following books: *Visual Studio 2019 In Depth* (BpB Publications) and *JavaScript for Gurus* (BpB Publications). He was the Technical Editor for *Professional C++*, 5th Edition (Wiley). He was a Microsoft Most Valuable Professional for .NET (2008–2017).

Acknowledgments

First, I'd like to thank my wife for her patience with me during the writing of this book.

I'd also like to thank the technical reviewer for his attention to detail and suggestions while reviewing this book. Thanks as well go to the team at Apress for helping to make the writing process a smooth experience.

Introduction

What This Book Is About

At a general level, software interoperability deals with how software components written in one language may be connected to other components written in other languages. More concretely, in C++ *Software Interoperability for Windows Programmers* we have a specific software ecosystem in mind. We want to connect a C++ codebase (our starting point) to client software written in three different languages: C#, R, and Python. This book has been written for those interested in learning how to build components that connect C++ to these languages and environments.

C++ is the language of choice for developing robust, scalable, and high-performance software. It offers both high-level software design capabilities through object-oriented, generic, and functional features as well as facilities for low-level memory manipulation. However, C++ is often awkward to connect to other languages. In fact, it doesn't communicate particularly well with clients even if these are written in C++. Consider by contrast how easily components written in different .NET languages can be put together and interoperate in different hosting environments. This book deals in a practical way with how C++ software components, specifically static and dynamic-link libraries, can be connected to components written in other languages. The overall aim is to demonstrate how to make the functionality offered by C++ code available to other clients and thereby leverage the power of C++.

This book is about developing the components that connect C++ libraries to client software written in other languages. It is not a book about the most performant or most up-to-date C++ code. These components form a translation or bridging layer and therefore will always have a performance cost. This is not a book about developing new applications. This book is more about how to connect possibly legacy systems with new(er) codebases. It deals with the in-between pieces of software that are not widely covered directly elsewhere. In this book, we are less interested in the specifics of the code itself and more interested in how the code is put together. We use examples from statistics, but these could equally well be from game engine development or quantitative finance. Our focus is on the wrapper components and how they connect to the different client languages.

Broadly speaking, this book looks at two main areas: firstly, the practicalities of building C++ components that target different languages, specifically C#, R, and Python. The main focus here is on the setup and structure of these middle layer components. We cover project types, project setup, and configuration. Secondly, this book is about the usage of frameworks that support interfacing to other languages. We make use of several such frameworks: C++/CLI (C++ adapted for the Common Language Infrastructure) for connecting to C# and the .NET universe, Rcpp to connect to the R language and environment. And lastly, for connecting to Python, we use CPython, Boost.Python, and PyBind. In each case, we will see how the frameworks help in the translation of types between C++ and the target language. We look at the specifics of how types from the C++ universe are converted to and from C#, R, and Python. We also touch on other areas that are important when developing wrapper components. We look at exception handling in the wrapper layer, unit testing, and also debugging. The focus here is on demonstrating in a realistic way some of the fundamental facilities offered by the frameworks.

It is worth emphasizing that there are advantages to developing separate wrapper components that interface with other client languages. From one point of view, legacy systems can be made more available and more open. This in turn improves the lifetime of those systems. And it allows us to retain the original code without having a costly rewrite. From another point of view, we can continue to use high-performance C++ code while at the same time reaping the benefits of perhaps more specialized languages (like R for data analysis) or perhaps languages with a possibly gentler learning curve (like Python). Apart from the benefits of the languages themselves, both R and Python have extensive libraries that support many different types of software development. By writing wrapper components, we can leverage C++ while at the same time taking advantage of what these languages offer.

What This Book Covers

Part 1 Foundations

Chapter 1 introduces the Software Interoperability project. Here, we cover some of the prerequisites. We describe the main features of the project and we give a high-level view of how the different components fit together.

Chapter 2 lays the foundations for the chapters to come. We introduce a simple C++ library of statistical functions that serves as the point of departure for the functionality that we want to expose to other clients. The library is simple enough to be readily understandable. The main focus is not on the (limited) functionality it offers but rather, in a general way, on what we want to expose to clients: built-in types, Standard Library types, and user-defined types. The statistical library is built as both a static library and a dynamic-link library for convenience. Following this, we take a brief look at two C++ clients: a simple console application that uses the static library and a Windows GUI application that uses the dynamic-link library. We see how simple it is to make the functionality available to C++ clients, but at the same time we see that if we want to expose the functionality outside the C++ world, it requires another layer and some different approaches.

Part 2 C++/CLI and .NET

Chapter 3 builds on these foundations. We'd like to make use of the statistics functionality offered by our C++ library. But what can we do if the client application is not written in C++ as in the previous chapter? One answer is to use C++/CLI to build a managed wrapper component for .NET.[1] .NET components are extremely versatile: we can easily drop them into a Windows WPF application or an ASP.NET web application, or have them available via Windows PowerShell. We see how the component we build in this chapter can be used anywhere within the extensive .NET framework.

Chapter 4 focuses on consuming the managed wrapper component. We illustrate some .NET features using a simple C# console application. After this, we take a short excursion into Excel as a client. Now that we have the statistical library available as a .NET component, we might like to be able to use it from Excel. Using Excel-DNA, we can easily connect our .NET wrapper component to Excel and take advantage of everything Excel offers as a hosting environment.

Part 3 R and Rcpp

Chapter 5 takes a similar approach to before. This time the question is what if we want to use the statistical functions in our C++ library from R? Again, we need to write a wrapper layer. This is somewhat more involved than previously. We need to set up R/RStudio

---

[1] As of .NET 2.0, Managed Extensions for C++ became known as C++/CLI (C++ adapted for the Common Language Infrastructure) and offers a redesign of the old syntax.

to compile a library into a package. R has quite specific requirements in terms of how packages should be built and managed, including what compiler should be used. We deal with the details here.

Chapter 6 takes the R package that we built in the previous chapter and exposes the functions via the Rcpp framework. Rcpp eases considerably the task of connecting C++ code to R. We investigate the Rcpp framework and write some R scripts to exercise our statistical functions. We also test out the statistical functions exercised from R.

Part 4 Python

Chapter 7 turns our attention to Python as the client language. In this chapter, we explore a basic approach to building a Python module. This low-level approach is instructive since we are dealing directly with Python objects and have to take care of all the low-level type conversion details ourselves. Here, we create a simple Python script that exercises the functions and classes in the statistical library. But it could just as easily be a micro-service built with Flask.

Chapter 8 extends the previous chapter. First, we use Boost.Python and then PyBind to illustrate different approaches to the wrapper layer. Boost.Python alleviates the burden of writing some translation code and allows us to expose C++ classes and functions to Python, at the cost of some complexity. We do the same using PyBind, a header-only library that simplifies exposing functions and classes in a wrapper component. In fact, we will see that the slightly thick wrapper we started with is slimmed down to almost nothing. PyBind does almost all the work. We just tell it what we want to expose. Now that we have a Python C++ extension module, we develop a Python script to measure the relative performance of using Python vs. C++.

Chapter 9 is the final chapter. We look back at what we've built: we now have working wrapper components that connect C++ to C#, R, and Python. And these should provide starting points for real-world development. The end goal is to broaden the architectural choices available when developing software systems. With these components you should be able to take a C++ codebase and make it available to client software written in C#, R, and Python.

Who This Book Is For

This book is aimed at intermediate-level software developers with some programming experience, particularly in C++ and particularly on Windows. We assume some familiarity with Windows static libraries, dynamic-link libraries, executables, and so on. You should be comfortable building software on Windows. No great expertise in C#, R, or Python is necessary, but a basic knowledge of, and some experience with, the languages and environments is useful. This book is not a primer for any of the languages we deal with and is not exhaustive or systematic in its treatment of either the languages or the frameworks. We let the C++ codebase drive what we need to use in a pragmatic way.

Throughout the book, we use a variety of tools, and you should be comfortable with these (or be able to use suitable alternatives). We use Visual Studio Community Edition 2019 for C++ related development. We use R/RStudio for R development (and Rtools for building the wrapper). We use CodeBlocks as a cross-platform development environment for building using gcc and related tools. We use Visual Studio Code for Python development.

This book is aimed at two slightly different audiences. On the one hand, the book is useful to C++ developers wanting to expand the types of software clients that can use their code. On the other hand, the book is also conceived for data scientists looking to leverage C++ code, either building their own codebases or making use of existing libraries. If you have ever wanted to connect some C++ code to .NET, perform some data analysis using C++ code from R, or build a Python extension module, this book is for you.

In both cases, the aim of this book is to broaden the architectural choices available when developing a loosely coupled software system. This book aims to make you comfortable developing and maintaining those in-between layers. If nothing else, I hope this book helps you get started if you are building components that make use of a C++ codebase and helps avoid some of the difficulties and traps you may find along the way.

PART I

Foundations

CHAPTER 1

Preliminaries

Introduction

This chapter introduces the Software Interoperability project. We take a brief look at the prerequisites first. This is followed by an overview of the project. Finally, we describe the main components of the projects and how these are organized.

Prerequisites

For the projects described in this book, the main tool we use is Visual Studio Community Edition 2019, with both C++17 and the latest .NET framework workloads installed. We also make use of Boost, specifically Boost version 1.76. The installation and setup of Boost is described in Appendix A. These form the core of the C++ development environment. In addition, for specific projects, we make use of GoogleTest and Excel-DNA. If needed, these can be installed or updated easily via the Package Manager from inside Visual Studio, and we will describe how to do this in the corresponding chapters.

For the development of R packages, we require RStudio Desktop (version 1.4.1106), R (version 4.0.3), and Rtools 4.0. All of these have downloadable Windows installers. Links to the latest (as of August 2021) distributions are as follows:

- RStudio: `www.rstudio.com/products/rstudio/download/`
- R: `https://cran.r-project.org/bin/windows/base/`
- Rtools: `https://cran.r-project.org/bin/windows/Rtools/`

Because these tools have different update cycles, it is useful to install them separately, rather than attempt to manage them together using Anaconda, for example.

© Adam Gladstone 2022
A. Gladstone, *C++ Software Interoperability for Windows Programmers*,
https://doi.org/10.1007/978-1-4842-7966-3_1

For Python development, we require Python 3.8. This is available from `www.python.org/downloads/release/python-380/`. There is no specific requirement for version 3.8. It just happened to be the latest version when this project got under way. As before, we prefer to manage this independently of, for example, Visual Studio Community Edition 2019. Managing the installations of tools ourselves gives us some more flexibility at the expense of a little more work keeping track of which versions we have installed.

In addition to the tools mentioned earlier, we use CodeBlocks as a cross-platform IDE. CodeBlocks comes with the MinGW toolset. We use CodeBlocks to manage and build a project using gcc, and we use Visual Studio Code as our environment for Python development. Neither of these are strictly required. For building with gcc, a distribution of mingw64 (`http://mingw-w64.org/doku.php`) is needed; beyond that, just a makefile is required. And for Python development, there are several alternatives to using Visual Studio Code (Jupyter, Idle, and Spyder, for example).

How to Use This Book

This book is about building software components. It is accompanied by a Visual Studio solution (*SoftwareInteroperability.sln*) that contains projects which build and test the wrapper components. By the end of the book, you will have working wrapper components that connect a simple C++ codebase to C# (and .NET), R, and Python. In the book, we approach this in stages, starting off by building the C++ library. Then, in the chapters that follow, we build the component wrappers and the demonstration programs. All the source code is present in the respective project files, but none of the binary components are built. We will give instructions on how the components are configured and built and explain features of the code and some of the design choices. To get the most out of this book, I recommend following this order as the later chapters need the C++ library. If this isn't built correctly, then the components that depend on it will not work. I would not recommend trying to build the solution "out of the box." There are dependencies that need to be installed and project settings that need to be configured. These are covered in the corresponding places in the book, and we will build and test the components as we cover them.

At the end of each of the chapters, from Chapter 2 through Chapter 8, there are exercises. The intention of the exercises is to provide some hands-on practice exposing some additional functionality that is part of the components that make up the Software Interoperability project. The exercises are intended to illustrate the types of issues covered in the respective chapters. The exercises are roughly graded with easier tasks coming first, followed by intermediate and advanced exercises. The exercises in the earlier chapters come with quite detailed instructions and hints, while later exercises leave out the detailed steps. Care has been taken to ensure that the exercises work correctly. There is a separate project zip file with all the tasks completed, tested, and working.

The Software Interoperability Project

The whole project can be downloaded as a zip file from the publisher's website. You should clone or unzip the contents to a directory called *SoftwareInteroperability*. As can be seen from Figure 1-1, the directory structure is quite flat.

Name	Size	Tags	Type
← → ∨ ↑	> This PC > DATA (D:) > Development > Projects > C++ > SoftwareInteroperability		
Common			File folder
Data			File folder
Exercises			File folder
packages			File folder
StatsATLCOM			File folder
StatsClient			File folder
StatsCLR			File folder
StatsCLR.UnitTests			File folder
StatsConsole			File folder
StatsDll			File folder
StatsExcel			File folder
StatsLib			File folder
StatsLibCB			File folder
StatsLibCM			File folder
StatsLibTest			File folder
StatsPython			File folder
StatsPythonBoost			File folder
StatsPythonPyBind			File folder
StatsPythonRaw			File folder
StatsR			File folder
StatsViewer			File folder
x64			File folder
NuGet.config	1 KB		XML Configuration File
SoftwareInteroperability.sln	15 KB		Visual Studio Solution

Figure 1-1. *Software Interoperability project directory structure*

The majority of the directories are the individual project directories containing project files, source code for the components, and tests. We describe these in some more detail in the following and in the subsequent chapters. In addition to the component project directories, there are several other directories worth highlighting. The *Common* directory contains two subdirectories: *include* and *source*. These contain the common header and source files that form the core of the C++ statistics library. The *packages* directory contains NuGet Package Manager information for GoogleTest and Excel-DNA. The *Data* directory contains a number of small datasets that we use at various points for testing. The files *xs.txt* and *ys.txt* are used throughout in various tests. The *us-mpg.txt* and *jp-mpg.txt* (and their equivalent *.csv* files) contain US and Japanese car petrol consumption data taken from the seaborn dataset `https://github.com/mwaskom/seaborn-data/blob/master/mpg.csv`. There is also an Excel workbook, *StatsCLRTest.xlsx,* containing tests of the StatsCLR component. We will cover this in Chapter 4. Lastly, the *\Exercises* directory contains a zipped copy of the solution file and all the projects with the completed exercises. The *\x64* directory (*debug* and *release*) contains the build artifacts.

The Projects

As can be seen from Figure 1-1, the Visual Studio solution *SoftwareInteroperability.sln* is located in the root directory of the project. It is useful to distinguish the Visual Studio projects from the other projects. In the Visual Studio solution, there are 12 projects in total. These are listed as follows with a short description of the project type.

The following are the C++ projects:

- **StatsCLR** is a C++/CLI wrapper. This component connects the C++ static library (StatsLib) to C# (and .NET).

- **StatsConsole** is a Windows console application. This application demonstrates the basic functionality of the statistics library with a minimal user interface.

- **StatsDll** is a dynamic-link library version of the statistics library.

- **StatsLib** is a static-link library version of the statistics library. Both this and the previous component share the same C++ source code.

- **StatsLibTest** is a Windows console unit-test application based on GoogleTest.

- **StatsPythonBoost** is a Boost.Python wrapper. This component connects C++ code to Python.

- **StatsPythonPyBind** is a PyBind wrapper. This component connects C++ code to Python.

- **StatsPythonRaw** is a CPython wrapper. This component connects C++ code to Python. The reason for having three components that do essentially the same thing is to cover, in a more general way, different approaches to connecting C++ to Python.

- **StatsViewer** is a Windows application built using MFC (Microsoft Foundation Classes). This application is used to demonstrate using the functionality available in the statistics library in a GUI application.

The following are the C# projects:

- **StatsCLR.UnitTests** is a C# unit test library that tests the basic statistics functionality from .NET.

- **StatsClient** is a basic C# console application that exercises the functionality from the statistics library via the StatsCLR wrapper component with a minimal user interface.

- **StatsExcel** is a C# library project. This component connects Excel to the StatsCLR wrapper component and allows Excel to use the functionality available in the statistics library.

Outside of the Visual Studio solution, there are three further projects.

- **StatsLibCB** is the CodeBlocks project that we use for building the R/RStudio ABI (Application Binary Interface) compatible static library.

- **StatsR** is the Rcpp wrapper component, built using Rtools via RStudio.

- **StatsPython** is a Visual Studio Code Python project containing a number of scripts that use the statistics library functionality.

Terminology

Throughout this book, we use the word "component" as a generic term encompassing any built unit of software (*lib*, *dll*, or *exe*). The wrapper components are all dynamic-link libraries from the point of view of Windows C++ projects. However, from the perspective of the client languages, they have different names, reflecting their different contents. For C++/CLI, we build a .NET assembly; for R, we build a package; and for Python, we build (extension) modules.

How the Projects Fit Together

The projects are organized to form a small environment that allows developing and building C++ components more or less easily for three different client languages: C#, R, and Python. Figure 1-2 illustrates how the components are related.

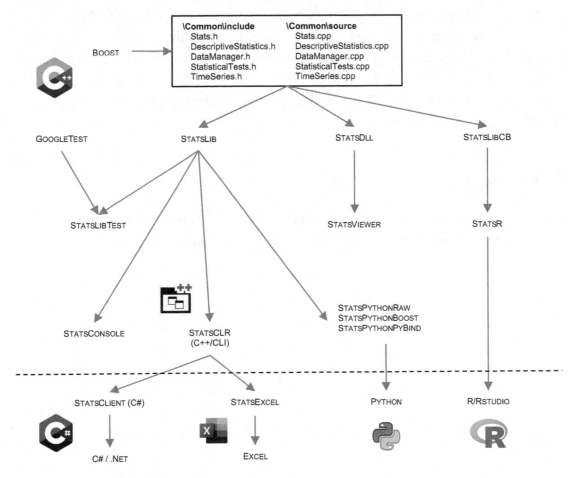

Figure 1-2. *The software ecosystem*

The central box at the top of the figure contains the C++ source code. Some of the code depends on the Boost libraries. The same source code is used to build three components: a static library (*StatsLib.lib*), a dynamic-link library (*StatsLib.dll*), and a static library built with gcc (*libStatsLib.a*).

Below these libraries are the wrapper components and the "client" applications that consume them. The applications StatsLibTest, StatsConsole, and StatsViewer link either with StatsLib or StatsDll and mostly serve to exercise and test the underlying functionality. The wrapper components StatsCLR and StatsPython link with StatsLib. The StatsR component links with the gcc compiled StatsLibCB.

The dotted line indicates the interface between the C++ components and the respective client languages. In the case of the C++/CLI assembly, we have two clients, a C# console application (StatsClient) and an assembly that connects to Excel (StatsExcel). In the case of R, the R package (StatsR) can be used with R, RGui, and RStudio either interactively or with R scripts. Similarly, the Python modules can be imported into any Python script or used interactively.

Summary

In this short chapter, we have given an overview of the Software Interoperability project organization. In the next chapter, we look at the C++ foundations in more detail.

## CHAPTER 2

C++ Components and C++ Clients

Introduction

In this chapter, we introduce the C++ codebase. This consists of a small set of statistical functions and classes. The intention is not to provide a fully fledged statistical library, but rather to provide some limited but useful functionality that we want to expose to clients. The functionality is only of interest insofar as it illustrates how we might expose it later to clients.

We start off by looking at the code, taking note of the functions we want to expose and the types that are used. In later chapters, we will see how the different language clients handle calling C++ functions and classes and the type conversions that are required. Following this we create two traditional Windows C++ components: a static library (*lib*) and a dynamic-link library (*dll*). This is traditionally how a lot of functionality is packaged on Windows platforms and exposed to Windows C++ clients. We look at both project settings and configuration. Finally, we present two client applications: StatsConsole and StatsViewer. Both these applications consume the functionality available in our small statistics library.

A Tour of the Source Code

The core C++ code is all located under the namespace Stats. It covers four main areas:

- Descriptive statistics: These are single values that summarize various aspects of a given dataset such as its central tendency and its spread. Descriptive statistics are a useful strategy in exploratory data analysis.

11

© Adam Gladstone 2022
A. Gladstone, *C++ Software Interoperability for Windows Programmers*,
https://doi.org/10.1007/978-1-4842-7966-3_2

- Linear regression: We implement a univariate linear regression function. Linear regression models a linear relationship between two variables. It can be used to fit a predictive model to an observed dataset of values.

- The Data Manager: This provides a simple caching mechanism for datasets. It enables users to load datasets from files, then store and retrieve them on demand.

- Statistical tests: The code here forms a class hierarchy for handling statistical hypothesis tests. We have classes to perform a student's t-test and an F-test. Roughly speaking, a t-test tests the difference between two means and an F-test tests whether two samples have the same variance.

We will describe each of these in turn in more detail. As pointed out earlier, the goal here is not to produce a fully fledged statistics library in C++. Rather, we want to have a codebase that is simple enough to understand but more realistic than a "Hello World" example in terms of the functionality that we want to expose to different target languages.

Descriptive Statistics

There are two parts to the descriptive statistics functionality: the summary statistics functions and the `GetDescriptiveStatistics` wrapper function. Inside the `Stats::DescriptiveStatistics` namespace are the individual functions. Figure 2-1 displays a list of the statistics we compute.

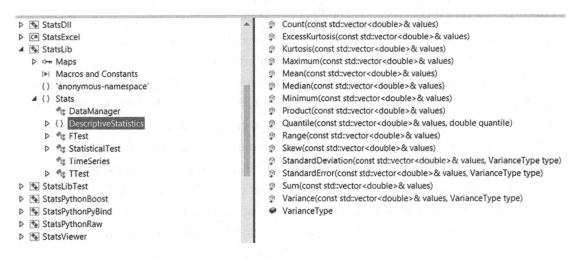

Figure 2-1. *View of the* `DescriptiveStatistics` *namespace*

As we can see from Figure 2-1, we compute a number of basic summary statistical measures. These cover measures of central tendency (mean and median) and measures of spread (standard deviation, variance, minimum, maximum, range, kurtosis, and skew). For computing the variance, standard deviation, and standard error, we have defined a `VarianceType` enumeration in order to distinguish between `population` or `sample` calculations.

The implementation of the functions has been kept deliberately simple. Listing 2-1 shows the code for computing the range.

Listing 2-1. Calculating the Range statistic

```
double Range(const std::vector<double>& values)
{
    check_empty_data(values);

    const auto [min, max] = std::minmax_element(std::begin(values), std::end(values));
    return (*max) - (*min);
}
```

Where possible, we use Standard Library facilities like std::minmax_element in the preceding listing and std::accumulate in other calculations. Also, in the preceding case, we take advantage of the C++17 structured bindings. At the top of the function, we check the input for empty values and throw an exception accordingly. We haven't made any attempt to optimize the functions. For example, we compute the Sum and the Mean separately, nor do we reuse the Mean function when computing the standard deviation. For the calculation of skew (a measure of how symmetric the dataset is) and both kurtosis (a measure related to how "fat" the tails of the data are) and excess kurtosis, we forward the calculations to the equivalent functions in boost::math::statistics.

The functions that compute the individual statistics are not exposed directly. Instead, we have chosen to wrap them in a single function call, as shown in Listing 2-2.

Listing 2-2. Two functions in the Stats namespace: GetDescriptiveStatistics and LinearRegression

```
Stats.h  ⊣ ✕
StatsLib              ▾  { } Stats          ▾  ᵠ  GetDescriptiveStatistics(const std::vector<double>& data, const std::vector<std::string>& keys)
    18      ⊟namespace Stats
    19       {
    20           // Retrieve a package of descriptive statistics for the input data
    21           STATSDLL_API std::unordered_map<std::string, double>
    22               GetDescriptiveStatistics(const std::vector<double>& data,
    23                   const std::vector<std::string>& keys = std::vector<std::string>());
    24
    25           // Perform simple univariate linear regression: y ~ x, (where y = B0 + xB1)
    26           STATSDLL_API std::unordered_map<std::string, double>
    27               LinearRegression(const std::vector<double>& xs, const std::vector<double>& ys);
    28       }
```

As can be seen from Listing 2-2, the GetDescriptiveStatistics function takes two parameters: the first is the input data, a vector of doubles. The second parameter is an optional list of keys. The keys are the name(s) of the statistics that we want to compute. If the keys are not provided or are empty, the default, then all the summary statistics are returned. The statistics are returned as a package of results. Listing 2-3 shows the implementation.

Listing 2-3. The implementation of `GetDescriptiveStatistics`

```
Stats.cpp  -□  ×
[■] StatsLib            ▼  { } Stats        ▼  ⊕ GetDescriptiveStatistics(const std::vector<double>& data, const std::vector<std::string>& keys)
  27  │         std::unordered_map<std::string, double>
  28  │             GetDescriptiveStatistics(const std::vector<double>& data,
  29  ⊟               const std::vector<std::string>& keys /* = std::vector<std::string>() */)
  30          {
  31              // Map of summary statistics functions
  32  ⊟           static const std::map<std::string,
  33                  std::function<double(const std::vector<double>& data)>> statistical_functions
  34  ⊞             { ... }
  77              std::unordered_map<std::string, double> results;
  78  ⊟           if (keys.empty())
  79              {
  80  ⊟               for (const auto& statistic : statistical_functions)
  81                  {
  82                      results[statistic.first] = statistic.second(data);
  83                  }
  84              }
  85  ⊟           else
  86              {
  87                  // Retrieve the requested statistics
  88  ⊟               for (const auto& key : keys)
  89                  {
  90                      const auto& it = statistical_functions.find(key);
  91  ⊟                   if (it == statistical_functions.end())
  92                      {
  93                          std::string invalidKey("Invalid key: " + key);
  94                          results[invalidKey] = 0.0;
  95                      }
  96  ⊟                   else
  97                      {
  98                          const auto& f = it->second;
  99                          results[key] = f(data);
 100                      }
 101                  }
 102              }
 103
 104              return results;
 105          }
```

The `GetDescriptiveStatistics` function (Listing 2-3) starts off by initializing a map of functions. We expand this code section later in the chapter. The code then creates an empty unordered map for the results. A map of results is convenient as it gives some flexibility if we wish to extend the statistics without impacting any client code. In the function body, we distinguish two cases. If the keys are empty, we trivially call each function in a map of `statistical_functions` and place the key and the corresponding result in the unordered map. In the case that the user has supplied keys, we iterate over them and check if the key name is valid. If so, we call the function, placing the result as before in the results map. If the key is not present, then we report this in the map and continue processing keys.

The individual statistics functions are declared and initialized in a local static `std::map` shown in Listing 2-4.

Listing 2-4. The map of statistical functions

```
Stats.cpp  ⊭  X
StatsLib              ▼  {} Stats            ▼  ⊕ GetDescriptiveStatistics(const std::vector<double>& data, const std::vector<std::string>& keys)
    31              // Map of summary statistics functions
    32              static const std::map<std::string,
    33                  std::function<double(const std::vector<double>& data)>> statistical_functions
    34          ⊟   {
    35                  { "Mean", Mean },
    36                  { "Median",  Median },
    37          ⊟     {
    38          ⊟         "StdDev.P", [](const std::vector<double>& data)
    39                              { return StandardDeviation(data, VarianceType::Population); }
    40                  },
    41          ⊟     {
    42          ⊟         "StdDev.S", [](const std::vector<double>& data)
    43                              { return StandardDeviation(data, VarianceType::Sample); }
    44                  },
    45          ⊞     { ... },
    49          ⊞     { ... },
    53          ⊞     { ... },
    57          ⊟     { "Skew", Skew },
    58                  { "Kurtosis", Kurtosis },
    59                  { "Kurtosis.XS", ExcessKurtosis },
    60                  { "Range", Range },
    61                  { "Minimum", Minimum },
    62                  { "Maximum", Maximum },
    63                  { "Sum", Sum },
    64          ⊞     { ... },
    68          ⊟     {
    69          ⊟         "Q1", [](const std::vector<double>& data)
    70                              { return Quantile(data, 0.25); }
    71                  },
    72          ⊟     {
    73          ⊟         "Q3", [](const std::vector<double>& data)
    74                              { return Quantile(data, 0.75); }
    75                  }
    76              };
```

The `statistical_functions` map defines a mapping from the named statistic to the function implementation and provides a simple function dispatch mechanism. The functions are typed as `std::function<double(const std::vector<double>& data)`. That is, they take a vector of `doubles` as an input parameter and return a `double`. In order to use the `VarianceType` parameter which we need for several of the statistics, we use anonymous lambdas as a convenient way to adapt the function call to the required type. Similarly, we use an anonymous lambda to call the `Quantile` function. We hardcode the second parameter corresponding to the quantile we want to expose. In this case, we only expose "Q1" (the 25% quantile) and "Q3" (the 75% quantile). However, together with the Median function and the Minimum and Maximum, we can provide a useful five-number summary of a dataset, for example.

Linear Regression

In the Stats namespace we have also declared a function LinearRegression. The implementation is shown in Listing 2-5.

Listing 2-5. Computing linear regression

```
Stats.cpp
StatsLib                        Stats                           LinearRegression(const std::vector<double>& xs, const std::vector<double>& ys)
114       //
115       std::unordered_map<std::string, double> LinearRegression(const std::vector<double>& xs, const std::vector<double>& ys)
116       {
117           using namespace Stats::DescriptiveStatistics;
118
119           check_same_size(xs, ys);
120
121           const double x_mean = Mean(xs);
122           const double y_mean = Mean(ys);
123           double ss_xy = 0;
124           double ss_xx = 0;
125
126           const std::size_t n = xs.size();
127
128           for (std::size_t i = 0; i < n; ++i)
129           {
130               ss_xx += (xs[i] - x_mean) * (xs[i] - x_mean);
131               ss_xy += (xs[i] - x_mean) * (ys[i] - y_mean);
132           }
133
134           const double b1 = ss_xy / ss_xx;
135           const double b0 = y_mean - b1 * x_mean;
136
137           std::unordered_map<std::string, double> results;
138
139           results["x-mean"] = x_mean;
140           results["y-mean"] = y_mean;
141           results["SS_xx"] = ss_xx;
142           results["SS_xy"] = ss_xy;
143           results["b0"] = b0;
144           results["b1"] = b1;
145
146           return results;
147       }
```

This function performs a simple univariate linear regression. At the start of the LinearRegression function, we check that the input vectors are the same size, and throw an exception if they are not. In this case, we make use of the Mean function to compute the coefficients. We compute the sums of squares of deviations from the respective means in the usual way. As before, the coefficients b0 and b1 as well as the standard values used in their calculation, are returned as a package with named results. This is somewhat more flexible than returning a std::pair<T> or a std::tuple<T>.

17

The Data Manager

The DataManager class is a utility class used to provide caching of named datasets. The class diagram is shown in Figure 2-2.

Figure 2-2. *The DataManager class diagram*

Managing datasets can be useful for client applications that do not have the facility to work with multiple datasets (e.g., the StatsConsole application). It permits loading and storing datasets which can be referenced later when performing statistical operations. In this context, a dataset is simply an association of a name with a vector of doubles. Datasets are stored in an unordered_map, keyed by name. We can see from Figure 2-2 that the DataManager class provides facilities to add, retrieve, count, list, and delete all the datasets. The code can be found in *DataManager.cpp*. In the client applications, we typically do not use this class (e.g., both Excel and R/RStudio provide better ways to manage datasets), though we can expose it to clients if required.

Statistical Tests

The StatisticalTest class hierarchy is shown in Figure 2-3.

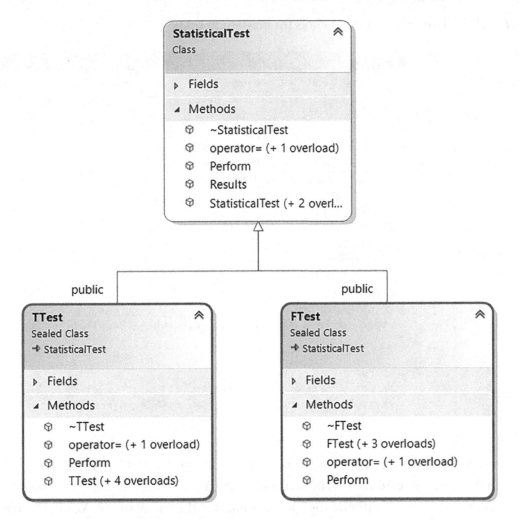

Figure 2-3. *The StatisticalTest class hierarchy*

As can be seen from Figure 2-3, the class hierarchy is composed of a base class StatisticalTest and two derived classes. The TTest class is used to perform student's t-tests and the FTest is used to perform F-tests. More classes could be added to the hierarchy if required, for example, a z-test class (one of the exercises) or a chi-squared test class.

The StatisticalTest class provides an abstract base class for performing statistical hypothesis tests. The base class declaration is shown in Listing 2-6. The default move and copy constructors and operators have been omitted.

Listing 2-6. The abstract base class for statistical tests

```
StatisticalTests.h  ⊣  ✕
⊞ StatsLib                        ▾    ⁴⁺ Stats::StatisticalTest              ▾
    25              // Base class for statistical testing: tTest, zTest, fTest ...
    26      ⊟       class STATSDLL_API StatisticalTest
    27              {
    28              public:
    29                  // Construction
    30                  StatisticalTest() = default;
    31
    32                  // Destructor
    33                  virtual ~StatisticalTest() = default;
    34
    35                  // Perform the statistical test
    36                  virtual bool Perform() = 0;
    37
    38                  // Retrieve the results
    39                  std::unordered_map<std::string, double> Results() const;
    40
    41      ⊞ ...
    53              protected:
    54                  // Collection of named results
    55                  std::unordered_map<std::string, double> m_results;
    56              };
```

The base class has a single pure virtual function, `Perform,` that is intended to
perform the required calculations in derived classes. Typically, in the derived classes, we
can use constructors to configure the specific details of the calculations. An alternative
approach would have been to define a further class hierarchy of test parameters that
the derived classes could operate on when performing tests. However, to keep things
simple, we just use the derived class constructors. This has the advantage that there are
no constraints on how the derived classes can be set up. The results of the statistical tests
are stored in the base class in a `std::unordered_map` and, as before, we store named
results. The set of results can be retrieved on demand using the `Results` function. In this
case, we do not give the user the choice of which specific results are retrieved.

Both the `TTest` and `FTest` classes are functionally quite similar, so we will only look
in detail at the `TTest` class. The class declaration is shown in Listing 2-7.

Listing 2-7. The derived class used to perform a student's t-test

```
67    class STATSDLL_API TTest final : public StatisticalTest
68    {
69        enum class STATSDLL_API TestType { Unknown, OneSample, TwoSample, NoSample };
70    public:
71        // Summary data: population mean, sample mean, sample standard deviation, sample size.
72        TTest(double mu0, double x_bar, double sx, double n);
73
74        // One-sample: population mean, sample.
75        TTest(double mu0, const std::vector<double>& x1);
76
77        // Two-sample
78        TTest(const std::vector<double>& x1, const std::vector<double>& x2);
79    ...
95        // Perform the statistical test
96        bool Perform() override;
97    private:
98        // mu0 unknown population mean
99        double m_mu0{ 0.0 };
100
101        // sample mean
102        double m_x_bar{ 0.0 };
103
104        // sample standard deviation
105        double m_sx{ 0.0 };
106
107        // sample size
108        double m_n{ 0.0 };
109
110        // Sample 1
111        std::vector<double> m_x1;
112
113        // Sample 2
114        std::vector<double> m_x2;
115
116        // Test type
117        TestType m_test_type{ TestType::Unknown };
118    };
```

The TTest class is declared final so we do not anticipate users deriving from it. As before, for brevity, the default functions and standard operators (copy and move assignment and so on) have been omitted from the listing. The constructors of the derived class are used to distinguish the three types of t-tests we are interested in. The summary data t-test accepts summary statistics as inputs. It uses a known population mean and summary measures for the sample mean, standard deviation, and the sample size. On the other hand, the one-sample t-test accepts a known population mean and a dataset. The dataset is used to compute the same summary measures (mean, standard deviation, and the sample size) that are used in the summary data t-test. The two-sample t-test compares two samples, specifically the sample means. There are a number of variations of the two-sample t-test (e.g., a paired t-test, which we do not support). In this version, we assume that both sample datasets have equal variances. The constructors are used to initialize the appropriate member variables and also to set the test type. No actual calculation is done until the `Perform` function is called. The `Perform` function checks the test type and computes the required values from the stored input data as required. Listing 2-8 shows the summary data and one-sample cases.

Listing 2-8. Calculations from a one-sample t-test

```
StatisticalTests.cpp  ☐ ✕
StatsLib                        ▼    (Global Scope)                                    ▼
    103        //
    104   ☐    bool TTest::Perform()
    105        {
    106            bool result = false;
    107
    108   ☐        if (m_test_type == TestType::NoSample || m_test_type == TestType::OneSample)
    109            {
    110   ☐            if (m_test_type == TestType::OneSample)
    111                {
    112                    m_n = static_cast<double>(m_x1.size());
    113                    m_x_bar = DescriptiveStatistics::Mean(m_x1);
    114                    m_sx = DescriptiveStatistics::StandardDeviation(m_x1, DescriptiveStatistics::VarianceType::Sample);
    115                }
    116
    117                const auto [t, p] = boost::math::statistics::one_sample_t_test(m_x_bar, m_sx * m_sx, m_n, m_mu0);
    118
    119                m_results["t"]      = t;
    120                m_results["pval"]   = p;
    121                m_results["df"]     = m_n - 1.0;
    122                m_results["x1-bar"] = m_x_bar;
    123                m_results["sx1"]    = m_sx;
    124                m_results["n1"]     = m_n;
    125
    126                result = true;
    127            }
    128   ⊞        else if (m_test_type == TestType::TwoSample) { ... }
    153
    154            return result;
    155        }
```

In Listing 2-8, we check the test type and compute the missing values: the sample size, the sample mean, and the standard deviation. If this had been a summary data t-test, these values would have been provided in the constructor arguments. `Perform` makes use of the `Mean` and `StandardDeviation` functions from the `DescriptiveStatistics` namespace. While the t-statistic is simple to calculate, the p-value requires a cdf (cumulative distribution function) for the student's t-distribution. For this, we make use of `boost::math::statistics`. Specifically, we use the `one_sample_t_test` and `two_sample_t_test` wrapper functions. The code can be found in *\boost\math\distributions\students_t.hpp*. The functions calculate the required statistics, the t-value and the p-value, and return the results in a tuple. The rest of the values are computed and returned as a package of named results.

The `FTest` class is structured in a similar way. There are two constructors: one that is used for summary data and a second one that is used when both sample datasets are supplied. The `Perform` function makes use of the `boost::math::fisher_f` distribution to compute the p-value. The results are returned as a package in a `std::unordered_map`.

Functions, Classes, and Type Conversion

Now that we have a good overview of the source code, we can see what we might need to expose to different language clients. We have the following functions: `GetDescriptiveStatistics` and `LinearRegression`; and the following classes: `DataManager` and `TTest`. We will also need to perform type conversion from one language to another. In general, we can distinguish three areas: conversions using built-in types, conversions using Standard Library types, and conversions involving user-defined types (C++ `classes` and `structs`). In terms of built-in types, we have the following: `bool`, `double`, and `std::size_t`. In terms of Standard Library types, we have `std::string`, `std::vector<double>`, `std::unordered_map<std::string, double>`, `DataSetInfo` which we have `typedef`'d as `std::pair<std::string, std::size_t>`, and `std::exception`. Finally, we have the user-defined types: `DataManager` and `TTest`. In the chapters that follow, we will see how these type conversions are handled using the different frameworks.

C++ Components

StatsLib

Now that we have seen the code, it is time to package it up into a library. StatsLib is the static library package for our statistical functions. In general, a static library is a useful way to reuse code and it is simple to incorporate inside other Windows executables.

Prerequisites

The only prerequisite for this project is having the Boost libraries installed. If you haven't installed boost, see Appendix A for how to do this. As mentioned before, we use Boost 1.76. This project references two Boost header files in *StatisticalTests.cpp*:

```
#include <boost/math/statistics/t_test.hpp>
#include <boost/math/distributions/fisher_f.hpp>
```

Also, in *DescriptiveStatistics.cpp* we need the following header for the skew and kurtosis measures:

```
#include <boost/math/statistics/univariate_statistics.hpp>
```

This only requires the Boost code. However, later on, we make use of Boost.Python which requires the Boost libraries to be built. It is worth getting this out of the way at this early stage, if possible.

Project Settings and Configuration

The initial StatsLib project properties are shown in Figure 2-4.

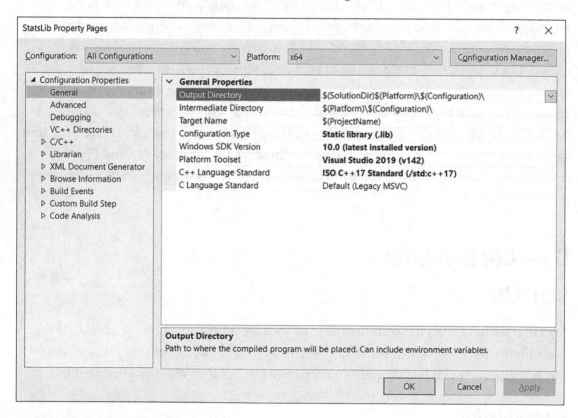

Figure 2-4. *StatsLib Property Pages*

At the top of the property pages, we set Configuration to All Configurations and set the Platform to x64. All the projects in this book target the x64 platform. This is convenient because we also depend on libraries that are built targeting x64. Specifically, we depend on Boost and Python having x64 builds of their libraries. In addition, we have

64-bit Excel installed and we use an x64 target when building our StatsExcel component using Excel-DNA. Depending on the clients, you may be able to change this to an x86/Win32 target and tweak the different project configurations. Throughout the book, we mainly deal with debug configurations. Again, this is just a convenience when we cover debugging. We can also build in Release x64. In the Configuration Properties, under General, we set the C++ Language Standard to ISO C++17 Standard (`/std:c++17`).

In the C/C++ node, under General, Additional Include Directories, we need to add the directory containing the Boost library. If you have previously set up the `BOOST_ROOT` environment variable, it will appear as `$(BOOST_ROOT)` under the Macros. Expand the Macros>> button and insert the variable if it is not present. Otherwise check that the path points to the Boost installation directory (in this case: *D:\Development\Libraries\boost_1_76_0*). This is shown in Figure 2-5.

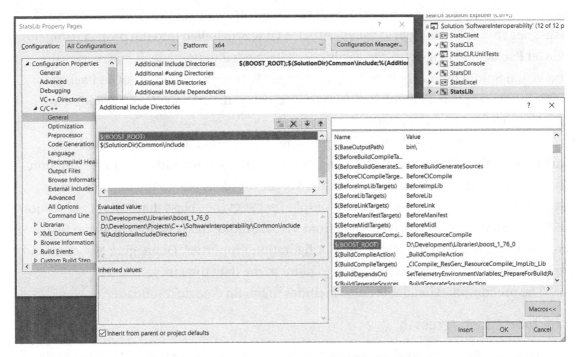

Figure 2-5. *Additional include directories and* $(BOOST\_ROOT)$

In addition, we need to reference the include directory with the header files for this project. In a "normal" project, this would be unnecessary since the project sources and includes would most likely be under the project directory. However, since we are sharing the same sources (and headers) for three different projects we need to tell the compiler where to find them. They are under the project directory: *$(SolutionDir)Common\include*. That is all the configuration that is needed.

Building and Testing the Project

With these settings in place, the project should build without warnings or errors. You might like to try this out. Any errors are likely to come from paths not being configured correctly, in particular, the path to the Boost headers and the project source and include files. If the project doesn't build, check these settings. Once the project is built, it is a good idea to test it.

StatsLibTest

StatsLibTest is a small console application which uses GoogleTest to provide an easy-to-use unit test framework for testing StatsLib. GoogleTest is a header-only unit-testing framework (https://github.com/google/googletest). Installing GoogleTest is described here (https://docs.microsoft.com/en-us/visualstudio/test/how-to-use-google-test-for-cpp?view=vs-2019). As it was installed into the project using the NuGet Package Manager, we can easily check if we need to upgrade the package using the Visual Studio menu Tools ➤ NuGet Package Manager ➤ Manage NuGet Packages for Solution. There isn't much in the way of project configuration. We have added a reference to the StatsLib project.

In this project, we make use of the precompiled header file. We have added includes for the STL libraries that we make use of and we have added a simple function to read data from a file and load it into a `std::vector<double>`. In the namespace `StatsLibTest::Utils`, we also have a simple `TestSettings` class that stores the location of the \Data directory. When running from Visual Studio, this is passed in as the first command-line argument. Under the Configuration Properties, Debugging ➤ Command Arguments we set $(SolutionDir)Data to point to the data directory.

The precompiled header file also includes the main GoogleTest header:

```
#include "gtest/gtest.h"
```

If you need to set additional test options, these can be found from the main menu under Tools ➤ Options ➤ Test Adapter for Google Test. The Google Test documentation has more information about these settings.

The rest of the files contain the unit tests for the StatsLib functions. They are organized to reflect the entities we want to test in StatsLib.

- *test_descriptive_stats.cpp*: Test cases for the descriptive statistics functions

- *test_data_manager.cpp*: Test cases for the data manager class

- *test_linear_regression.cpp*: Test cases for the simple linear regression function

- *test_statistical_tests.cpp*: Test cases for the t-test and F-test hypothesis testing classes

The tests themselves follow the *arrange-act-assert* pattern. Listing 2-9 shows the code that tests the values returned from the one-sample t-test.

Listing 2-9. Testing the one-sample t-test

```
test_statistical_tests.cpp  ⊣ X
StatsLibTest              ▼   (Global Scope)                          ▼  ● TEST(StatisticalTests, OneSampleTTest)
    31
    32      □ TEST(StatisticalTests, OneSampleTTest)
    33        {
    34      ⊞      // ...
    37
    38           // Arrange
    39           const std::string weight_data = testSettings.GetDataDirectory() + "\\weight.txt";
    40
    41           std::vector<double> x1 = ReadData(weight_data);
    42
    43           TTest statistical_test(25.0, x1);
    44
    45           // Act
    46           const bool result = statistical_test.Perform();
    47           const auto results = statistical_test.Results();
    48
    49           // Assert
    50           EXPECT_EQ(result, true);
    51           EXPECT_NEAR(results.at("t"), -9.0783, 1e-4);
    52           EXPECT_NEAR(results.at("pval"), 7.9531e-06, 1e-6);
    53           EXPECT_DOUBLE_EQ(results.at("df"), 9.0);
    54           EXPECT_NEAR(results.at("x1-bar"), 19.25, 1e-2);
    55           EXPECT_NEAR(results.at("sx1"), 2.00291, 1e-5);
    56           EXPECT_DOUBLE_EQ(results.at("n1"), 10);
    57        }
```

The test in Listing 2-9 reads the data first, then constructs a TTest instance with the corresponding parameters (a known population mean and the dataset). It calls Perform followed by Results. The results are checked against the expected values using the macros EXPECT_EQ, EXPECT_NEAR with a tolerance and EXPECT_DOUBLE_EQ. We also test the case where the one-sample t-test throws an exception due to empty input data. This is shown in Listing 2-10.

Listing 2-10. Checking exception handling

```
test_statistical_tests.cpp  ⊕ ×
StatsLibTest          ▼   (Global Scope)                          ▼ ● TEST(StatisticalTests, OneSampleTTestNoData)
   58
   59   ⊟ TEST(StatisticalTests, OneSampleTTestNoData)
   60     {
   61         // Arrange
   62         std::vector<double> x1{ };
   63
   64         TTest statistical_test(25.0, x1);
   65
   66         // Act / Assert
   67         EXPECT_THROW(statistical_test.Perform(), std::invalid_argument);
   68
   69         const auto results = statistical_test.Results();
   70
   71         // Assert
   72         EXPECT_EQ(results.size(), 0);
   73     }
```

In Listing 2-10, the TTest instance is constructed with empty data and throws std::invalid_argument as expected, hence the test passes.

Building, Running, and Checking the Results

StatsLibTest should build and run without warnings or errors. The results appear summarized on the console. There should be no test errors. To see the results output to a file, open the Project Properties and select Debugging, Command Arguments. Add the following line:

```
--gtest_output=xml:<your path>\SoftwareInteroperability\StatsLibTest\
Output\StatsLibTest.xml
```

Overall, the StatsLibTest project provides the testing support we need if we want to extend the functionality offered by the statistics library.

StatsDll

StatsDll is a dynamic-link library housing our statistical functions. It contains the same source code as StatsLib, but in this case, we package the functionality as a *dll*.

Project Settings and Configuration

In the Visual Studio solution, under the project settings, we can see that in the Configuration Properties, under General, the Configuration Type is set to Dynamic Library (*dll*). The Additional Include Directories are set up in the same way as before. They reference both the Boost libraries and the directory with our headers.

```
$(BOOST_ROOT)
$(SolutionDir)Common\include
```

The only other difference between this and the static library is in the Preprocessor Definitions under Configuration Properties ➤ C/C++. The Visual Studio project template for Windows *dll*s adds a definition for <PROJECTNAME>_EXPORTS to the defined preprocessor macros. In this example, Visual Studio defines STATSDLL_EXPORTS when the StatsDll DLL project is built.

In the code, we conventionally define an API symbol, as Listing 2-11 shows.

Listing 2-11. Standard preprocessor definitions

```
Stats.h ↔ ×  DataManager.h
StatsDll                     ▼   (Global Scope)                                    ▼
    6      //
    7      #ifdef DYNAMIC
    8      #   ifdef STATSDLL_EXPORTS
    9      #       define STATSDLL_API __declspec(dllexport)
   10      #   else
   11      #       define STATSDLL_API __declspec(dllimport)
   12      #   endif
   13      #else
   14      #   define STATSDLL_API
   15      #endif
```

If we are building a static library (DYNAMIC is not defined), then we do not care about the __declspec(...) directives, and the STATSDLL_API symbol evaluates to empty. On the other hand, if we are building a dynamic library (with DYNAMIC defined in the project preprocessor definitions), then we identify functions that are exported using the symbol STATSDLL_EXPORTS. When the STATSDLL_EXPORTS macro is defined, the STATSDLL_API macro sets the __declspec(dllexport) modifier on the function declarations. This modifier tells the compiler and linker to export a function or variable from the DLL for use by other applications. In Listing 2-2, for example, we identify the two functions `GetDescriptiveStatistics` and `LinearRegression` for export when building the StatsDll component. When `STATSDLL_EXPORTS` is not defined, for example, when the header file is included by a client application, `STATSDLL_API` applies the `__declspec(dllimport)` modifier to the declarations, which indicates that we want to import the function or variable in our application.

Building and Testing the Project

We can now build the StatsDll project. It should build without warnings or errors. If there are errors, the most likely source is the path settings, so you should check these. You can see the functions and classes that have been exported using a tool like *Depends.exe* or *dumpbin.exe* if you prefer. Since the underlying code is the same as the StatsLib, we do not need to test it separately.

So far, in this chapter, we have built two traditional C++ components based on the same source code: a static library and a dynamic-link library. These components house the functionality that we will be making available to various non-C++ language clients in the forthcoming chapters. The reason for building both sorts of C++ components is that they are typical ways of packaging functionality on Windows.

From the point of view of the components that we build in this book, there is very little difference between linking to a static library or a dynamic library. However, in a more realistic scenario, for example when developing a middle-layer component that connects a legacy C++ codebase to Python, you cannot choose how the existing functionality is presented to you. It may be in a static library or it may be in a dynamic-link library (it may also be in a header-only library, or it may be embedded in an executable, but we don't deal with either of these cases in this book). The components that we build in Chapters 3 to 8 will work equally well when connecting to C++ static libraries or dynamic-link libraries. However, for the purposes of exposition, we often use the static library StatsLib.

C++ Clients

Introduction

In this section, we present briefly two client applications: StatsConsole and StatsViewer. Both these applications consume the functionality available in our small statistics library. Apart from being a useful test of how the functions can be used, it is also instructive in terms of how C++ clients connect to C++ components.

StatsConsole

StatsConsole is a typical Windows console application. The application consists of a menu manager. This displays the menu items on the console output and manages the function dispatch based on user input selection. Figure 2-6 shows a typical example session performing a t-test from summary data and displaying the results.

```
 D:\Development\Projects\C++\SoftwareInteroperability\x64\Debug\StatsConsole.exe        —    □    ×

1. Enter Console Data
2. Load Data from File
3. List Data Sets
4. Display Data
5. Descriptive Statistics
6. Linear Regression
7. Summary Data T-Test
8. One-sample T-Test
9. Two-sample T-Test
10. Summary Data F-Test
11. Two-sample F-Test
12. Quit
Enter Selection> 7
===================Summary Data T-Test====================
Population mean: mu0> 5
Sample mean: x-bar> 9.26146
Sample stdev: s> 0.227881e-1
Sample size: n> 195
             t:        2611.37
          pval:        0
            df:        194
        x1-bar:        9.26146
          sx1:         0.0227881
           n1:         195
=========================================================

1. Enter Console Data
2. Load Data from File
3. List Data Sets
```

Figure 2-6. *A typical session in StatsConsole*

Other sessions might consist of loading one or more datasets from a file, caching these by adding them with a name to the data manager, then retrieving descriptive statistics and performing a linear regression.

StatsConsole links to the static library StatsLib. All we need to do for this to work is to reference the header files and add the corresponding *lib* file (or we can just add a project reference) and the functions and classes are immediately available to us.

StatsViewer

Compared to StatsConsole, the StatsViewer application is somewhat more sophisticated. It is a typical menu-driven Windows MFC application. From a user-interface point of view, it uses a Single Document Interface (SDI). The main view consists of two list controls. The list control on the left displays the contents of any datasets that have been loaded. An Index column is automatically added for reference. The list control on the right displays the results of the Statistics menu operations. Figure 2-7 shows a typical session after loading a dataset and retrieving the descriptive statistics. The results can be copied to the clipboard if required.

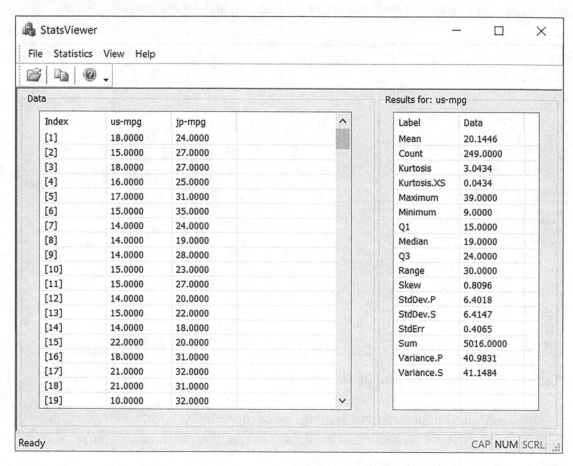

Figure 2-7. *StatsViewer displaying the descriptive statistics for the us-mpg dataset*

In this application, we connect to the statistics functions using StatsDll. Apart from referencing the header files and including the *dll* (or referencing the project), we don't need to do any further configuration. In both the applications, all the exported functions in the StatsLib or StatsDll are available and can be used seamlessly.

In both these examples, we have seen how to make use of functionality housed in C++ components. We simply add the components to a C++ executable host. Together, the applications serve to illustrate how we might make use of functionality packaged in real C++ components in a realistic way.

There are, however, some limitations in the respective hosting environments. Exposing the functionality via a Windows console application is somewhat restrictive. It limits the choice of data input, for example. Even with the more fully featured MFC application, we can see various issues. The tabular display leaves quite a lot to be desired. The list control is not necessarily the best choice to display a grid of data. No doubt there are many alternatives, including ActiveX grid components that could do this better. However, what if we want to plot the data, perhaps a box plot of the *us-mpg* vs. *jp-mpg* datasets? While the statistics library provides functionality for performing a t-test of this data, we would have to look elsewhere for doing any plotting. Again, there are other components that can do this (gnuplot, for example). However, the interface to connect this to our statistical library is quite specific to gnuplot, and not easily generalizable.

More fundamentally, however good the C++ language is for performing calculations, threading, or concurrent processing, and however extensive the universe of libraries is, we would still like to be able to use the code in other sorts of client software. The issue centers around not just the limitations of what we can achieve within an application, but also the limitations on how this functionality interoperates with other components.

With the functionality inside a static or a dynamic-link library, the question arises: How do you make it available, either to other languages or other types of clients? Of course, we could have packaged the functionality in a different way. We could have built this into a header-only library. This is undoubtedly easier to distribute than a dynamic-link library and more convenient to use. But again, this is only convenient in the C++ universe. We would still be left with the same question: what if we want to use this with a machine learning library or with an R script, or from a Python script using Pandas and NumPy?

One alternative that we might have considered is developing a COM wrapper. We could then use the functionality from a VBScript, for example. Or we could use the component in .NET, taking advantage of the .NET Interop to generate the required "wrapper" code from the embedded type information. Indeed, this is similar to the approach we adopt using C++/CLI in Chapter 3. However, COM belongs to an older technology and requires familiarity with topics such as component registration, marshalling, and threading models. Developing a COM wrapper is more involved. This is partly because the frameworks (MFC and ATL, for example), despite having been around for a while, are less well evolved or coherent, and also because they offer quite low-level facilities, leaving you to do more of the work.

Arguably, much of the modern component development in .NET addresses and solves issues that originated with COM (e.g., registration, type information, versioning of components, marshalling, threading models, and so on). In order to make the functionality in StatsLib available to other languages and clients, we need to develop components that bridge this gap and can form part of a system of loosely coupled components in their respective environments (.NET, R, and Python).

Summary

In this chapter, we have laid the foundations for developing the components that connect to other languages. We have looked at the source code and built two Windows libraries that package the functionality. We have seen how to use these C++ components in two different clients: a simple console application and a more fully featured Windows GUI application. This brings us to the edge of the large but finite C++ universe. There are a much greater range of potential client applications that could make use of the functionality in our library, using a wider range of technologies and languages. If we want to go any further – WPF (Windows Presentation Foundation) applications, web applications, micro-services, a Shiny tableau built on R, or a machine learning application in Python to name but a few, we will need to build additional components that perform the appropriate translations for these clients housed in whatever modules are required. The intention of this book is to show you how to do this for C#, R, and Python.

It would be ideal to be able to write a component in C++ and simply "drop" it into a C# application, or call the functionality directly from R or Python. But doing this is not possible (as far as I know), so we have to build the components that allow us to do this. The rest of this book is about building and using those components.

Additional Resources

The following links contain some useful background information on the topics covered in this chapter:

- A useful resource covering all the statistics we use here is the Engineering Statistics Handbook: `www.itl.nist.gov/div898/ handbook/index.htm`. This provides detailed definitions, formulas, and explanations of the statistics.

- For more information on the functionality provided by `boost::math::statistics`, I recommend the math toolkit and the univariate statistics library documentation at `www.boost.org/doc/ libs/1_77_0/libs/math/doc/html/math_toolkit/univariate_ statistics.html` and `www.boost.org/doc/libs/1_77_0/libs/ math/doc/html/statistics.html`.

- The GoogleTest unit testing framework is documented here: `https://github.com/google/googletest`. There are a number of useful references to both general testing practices and specific features of GoogleTest.

- The approach for using the COM interop in .NET is described here: `https://docs.microsoft.com/en-us/dotnet/standard/native- interop/cominterop`.

Exercises

The exercises in this chapter extend the C++ codebase. There are three main sets of changes that we will deal with. Firstly, we look at adding some more results to the descriptive statistics and the linear regression functions. Secondly, we add a z-test class to the `StatisticalTest` class hierarchy. Finally, we incorporate a `MovingAverage` function from a `TimeSeries` class. The functionality that is added here will be used in later exercises where we make this available to the different client languages.

1) In addition to the dedicated `Median` function, there is a more general `Quantile` function. The `Median` function is therefore unnecessary. In the functions mapping, replace the function `Median` with the anonymous lambda using the `Quantile` function with the `quantile=0.5`. Keep the original "Median" label.

Alternatively, add a new function mapping labelled: "Q2". This will be incorporated into the results package, so can be inspected immediately.

- After rebuilding the StatsLib project, the StatsDll project, and the StatsLibTest project, check that all the tests pass. You should not need to add a separate test for this. All the test results should remain the same. Rebuild both the StatsConsole and the StatsViewer. Check that the expected results are displayed.

2) Add support for computing the correlation coefficient r and the r^2 coefficient as part of the LinearRegression results. The correlation coefficient measures the correlation between the observed values and the predicted values. The r^2 statistic indicates how much variation is explained by the regression coefficients.

Using the same naming convention for the sums of squares that we use in the code, the calculation is

```
const double r = ss_xy / std::sqrt(ss_xx * ss_yy);
```

- Add the calculation for r^2. Also, add the new coefficients to the results package.

- In the StatsLibTest project, in the test file *test_linear_regression.cpp*, in the test fixture TestLinearRegression, add code to test the results. Rebuild the StatsLibTest project. Check that all the tests pass.

- Run the StatsConsole application. Load the *xs* and *ys* datasets (the same datasets that are used in the tests). Check the regression and correlation coefficients are displayed. Run a similar test using the StatsViewer application.

3) In the StatsLib project, there is a class called TimeSeries that is already included in the sources. It has a single function: MovingAverage. There is already a test for this function: TestMovingAverage in *test_time_series.cpp*.

- Add support for a "Moving Average" menu item in the StatsConsole project.

To visually inspect the results, you can run a StatsConsole session loading *moving_average.txt* and setting the window as 3. This is the same data that is used in the TestMovingAverage test.

4) Add a z-test class to the statistical tests class hierarchy. A z-test is a method to determine whether two sample means are approximately the same or different when their variance is known and the sample size is large (typically ≥30). The z-test is more fully described here: `https://en.wikipedia.org/wiki/Z-test`.

For this statistical test, we only use the Boost functionality `boost::math::cdf`. The `ZTest` class is derived from the `StatisticalTest` base class. The z-test is functionally (not statistically) almost identical to the t-test. The only change is in the underlying distribution. For this exercise, we can clone the t-test code to implement a z-test class that works in an almost identical fashion. This also simplifies the enhancements we will make to the upcoming wrapper components. It should be emphasized that this is a convenience. There are several better design alternatives, but these would involve many more changes both here and later on. So, to keep things simple, we will create a new `ZTest` class similar to the `TTest` class and use the Boost implementation.

Follow these steps to implement the z-test functionality:

- Derive a new `ZTest` class and add the class definition to *StatisticalTests.h*.

- In *StatisticalTests.cpp*, add the include file:

  ```
  #include <boost/math/statistics/z_test.hpp>
  ```

- Add the class implementation to *StatisticalTests.cpp*. Implement the constructors in the same way as the t-test: that is, we can have z-test from data, a one-sample z-test and a two-sample z-test.

- Implement the function `Perform`. We need to make a couple of changes here:

  - Add a declaration for the normal distribution at the top of the function:

    ```
    boost::math::normal dist;
    ```

  - Compute the test statistics for both the one-sample and two-sample cases as follows (using the same naming convention we used for the t-test):

```
// One-sample case
const double t = (m_x_bar - m_mu0) / (m_sx / std::sqrt(m_n));
// ...
// Two-sample case
const double t = (mean1 - mean2) / std::sqrt((((sd1 * sd1) /
n1) + ((sd2 * sd2) / n2)));
```

- Add code to both the test types that obtains a p-value:

    ```
    double p = 2.0 * boost::math::cdf(boost::math::complement(dist,
    test_statistic));
    ```

- The implementation of the Results function is already handled in the base class. In this case, we just add the same values to the results package. We change the name of the test statistic from "t" to "z" to reflect the fact that we have performed a z-test. We can also remove the "df" (degrees of freedom) result as it is not used for the z-test.

- Rebuild the StatsLib project and the StatsDll project. Obtain test data for three cases: z-test from data, one-sample z-test, and two-sample z-test. In StatsLibTest, add appropriate tests.

PART II

C++/CLI and .NET

CHAPTER 3

Building a C++/CLI Wrapper

Introduction

In this chapter, we build our first wrapper component. We use C++/CLI which allows .NET clients to call C++ code. We take StatsLib, our small library of statistical functions that we built in Chapter 2, and expose the functionality via C++/CLI.

The intention of this chapter is to create a fully working and usable .NET component, albeit with limited functionality. The reason for this is to cover as many of the technical details as possible in a realistic context. On the other hand, this chapter is not a reference manual for C++/CLI. The C++/CLI Language Specification is a large document specifying requirements for implementations of the C++/CLI binding. It covers all the features of the language in depth. Furthermore, we are not aiming to be exhaustive in our coverage. We limit ourselves to what is required by the specifics of the component we are developing. We let the code, limited as it is, determine the topics we cover. The Additional Resources section at the end of the chapter provides links to topics that are covered in more detail elsewhere.

The underlying statistics library (StatsLib) that we want to wrap has just enough functionality to make it interesting and also to serve as a point of departure for further development. This chapter aims to demonstrate a particular architectural choice in a realistic enough way so as to be useful. By writing a small component to connect two languages, we are able to decouple the statistical functionality from the client usage. Furthermore, this chapter demonstrates the internal design that is involved in a C++/CLI wrapper, separating the code that exposes functions and classes from the layer that is concerned with converting types between the managed and unmanaged worlds.

© Adam Gladstone 2022
A. Gladstone, *C++ Software Interoperability for Windows Programmers*,
https://doi.org/10.1007/978-1-4842-7966-3_3

Prerequisites

C++/CLI support

The main prerequisite for this project is to have installed support for C++/CLI. C++/CLI support is an additional workload in Visual Studio Community 2019 and can be installed using the Visual Studio Installer. If you already have it installed, you can skip this section. If not, launch the installer and, from the "Desktop development with C++" section on the right, select "C++/CLI support". This is shown in Figure 3-1.

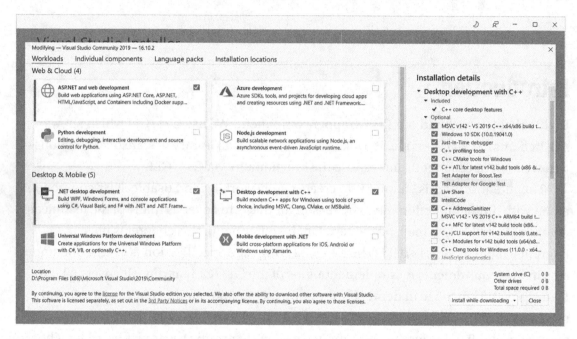

Figure 3-1. *Installing C++/CLI support*

After this, select your preferred download and installation options and install the workload.

StatsCLR
Project Settings

The StatsCLR project was created with the CLR Class Library (.NET Framework) project template targeting C++. We could equally have used the CLR Empty Project (.NET Framework). However, the former generates the precompiled header files and the *AssemblyInfo.cpp* attributes which we use.

Table 3-1 summarizes the project settings.

Table 3-1. *StatsCLR project settings*

Settings		
Tab	Property	Value
General	C++ Language Standard	ISO C++17 Standard (/std:c++17)
Advanced > C++/CLI Properties	Common Language Runtime Support	Common Language Runtime Support (/clr)
C/C++ > General	Additional Include Directories	*$(SolutionDir)Common\include*

From Table 3-1, we have set the C++ Language Standard to C++17. This is for consistency with the StatsLib project. Next, we have set the Additional Include Directories. We require a reference to the C++ code so we set this to *$(SolutionDir) Common\include*. We have also added a reference to the StatsLib project to the project references node. The most important setting for this project is the Common Language Runtime Support. This is shown in Figure 3-2.

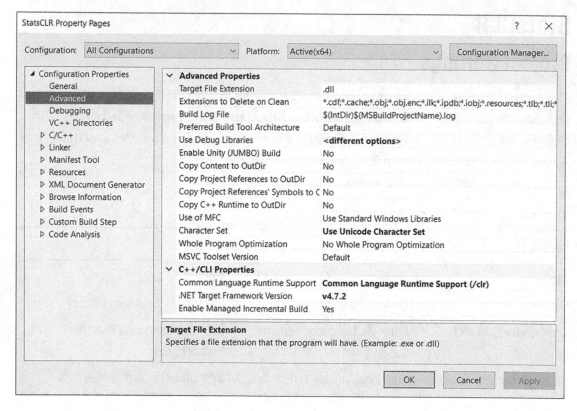

Figure 3-2. *Setting CLR support*

The */clr* switch is the default option for C++/CLI projects. The switch enables the use of the managed runtime. C++/CLI projects are sometimes referred to as mixed assemblies as they contain both unmanaged machine instructions and MSIL (Microsoft Intermediate Language) instructions.[1] From a practical point of view, this arrangement allows us to write components using a mixture of .NET and native C++ code. Use of the managed runtime means that we can add references to other .NET framework components to the project and with the using directive we can access the full range of .NET functionality. For example, in this project, we make use of .NET generics by including the following line:

```
using namespace System::Collections::Generic;
```

---

[1] For those interested in the details, the intermediate language disassembler tool (ildasm.exe) allows you to explore the generated IL code.

Rather than developing a separate clr-compliant wrapper component from scratch as we do here, there are other architectural choices. We could use the StatsLib project directly, and recompile it with the */clr* switch. However, this approach depends to some extent on what dependencies we have introduced in the library (for example, in our case, we depend on the Boost libraries). This may cause issues at compile-time. Another alternative is to compile functions as managed or unmanaged using the corresponding #pragma directive within the same file.[2] We do not use either of these approaches. Instead, we prefer to keep things simple. Therefore, we keep the underlying native C++ library separate from the wrapper component.

Code Organization

The StatsCLR project consists of the following files with a brief description of what they contain:

- *Conversion.h/.cpp* This contains the type conversion functions.

- *DataManager.h/.cpp* This contains the managed wrapper around the native C++ DataManager class.

- *Statistics.h/.cpp* This contains the managed wrapper around the native C++ statistical test classes.

- *pch.h/.cpp* This is the precompiled header file.

- *Resource.h* A resource file for the project.

- *AssemblyInfo.cpp* This contains basic metadata about this assembly: name, description, version, etc.

The code is organized into two separate namespaces under the StatsCLR project namespace: Functions and Conversion. When developing a wrapper layer, it is helpful to separate these two tasks. The Functions namespace organizes the code that is calling the functions and classes. In this case, we will look at the Statistics class, then the DataManager, and finally the StatisticalTest classes. The Conversion namespace contains the type conversion code. This gives us a degree of flexibility in how we choose to handle the conversions.

---

[2] This approach is described here: https://docs.microsoft.com/en-us/cpp/preprocessor/managed-unmanaged?view=msvc-160.

The Statistics Class

We start by looking at the `Statistics` class. The code is reproduced in Listing 3-1.

Listing 3-1. The `Statistics` class declaration

```
Statistics.h    ⊣  ×
StatsCLR                    ▾    (Global Scope)                          ▾
     1      #pragma once
     2
     3    □ using namespace System;
     4      using namespace System::Collections::Generic;
     5      using namespace System::Text;
     6
     7    □ namespace StatsCLR
     8      {
     9          // Performs statistical operations
    10    □     public ref class Statistics abstract sealed
    11          {
    12          public:
    13              // Return descriptive statistics for the input data
    14              static Dictionary<String^, double>^ DescriptiveStatistics(List<double>^ data);
    15
    16              // Return descriptive statistics for the input data
    17              static Dictionary<String^, double>^ DescriptiveStatistics(List<double>^ data, List<String^>^ keys);
    18
    19              // Perform simple univariate linear regression: y ~ x, (y = B0 + xB1)
    20              static Dictionary<String^, double>^ LinearRegression(List<double>^ xs, List<double>^ ys);
    21          };
    22      }
```

There are several features of this code worth highlighting. We declare `Statistics` as a `ref class`. A `ref class` is a C++/CLI class. This creates a reference type whose lifetime is automatically managed by the CLR. If you want to make a class that is usable from C#, you would typically create a `ref class`. This can then be called using C#'s `new` operator, for example. Similarly, a `ref struct` does exactly the same thing, but with C++'s standard `struct` default accessibility rules. In this case, since we only have static functions, there is no constructor or destructor. Next, the `abstract` keyword declares this class as a type that can be used as a base type, but which cannot be instantiated. Following this, the `sealed` keyword (for `ref` classes) indicates that a virtual member cannot be overridden, or that a type cannot be used as a base type. Therefore, we cannot derive from this class. It is similar to the `final` keyword on C++ classes. The functions can be called from C# code as follows:

```
List<double> xs = new List<double> {0,1,2,3,4,5,6,7,8,9};
Dictionary<string, double> results = Statistics.DescriptiveStatistics(xs);
```

The final feature worth noting are the reference handles, denoted by the ^ in C++/CLI. This can be thought of as an opaque pointer type. What is more important is that the memory it refers to is managed. Here we need to distinguish between unmanaged memory (memory returned to us from C++'s `operator new`) which comes from the CRT (C-Runtime Library) heap, and managed memory, which is administered by the .NET runtime and recovered by the GC (Garbage Collector). Letting the GC manage memory on our behalf simplifies our code to some extent. Managed memory does not need to be explicitly deleted. On the other hand, we need to be aware that the managed memory that is being referenced doesn't have a fixed address and may be moved around. As a result, special consideration needs to be given when dealing with memory in C++/CLI.

Parameters and Return Values

In the functions mentioned earlier, we are passing our parameters as a generic list `List<double>^`. This is a choice that we have made. Given that the underlying type is a `std::vector<double>`, this seems reasonable. We could have chosen an array type for example or some other type that better suits our purposes. The important point here is that it is a choice. Given this, we will then need to convert `List<double>^` to `std::vector<double>`. Similarly, the return type for the `LinearRegression` function is a dictionary of `string` keys and `double` values. It is declared as `Dictionary<String^, double>^`. As before, we have tried to keep close to the underlying type, `std::unordered_map<std::string, double>`. However, there are other choices. We could have used `List<Tuple<String^, double>>` and in some ways this better represents a `std::unordered_map` because it does not impose any ordering, unlike the `Dictionary` collection.

Descriptive Statistics

The implementation of the function `DescriptiveStatistics` is quite straightforward. It is shown with the overloaded version in Listing 3-2.

Listing 3-2. The implementation of the `DescriptiveStatistics` function and the overloaded version

```
Statistics.cpp  ⊣  ×  Statistics.h
StatsCLR                        ▼   (Global Scope)                              ▼
    13    □namespace StatsCLR
    14     {
    15    ⊞     // ...
    18    □     Dictionary<String^, double>^ Statistics::DescriptiveStatistics(List<double>^ data, List<String^>^ keys)
    19          {
    20              STATS_TRY
    21              std::vector<double> _data = Conversion::ListToVector(data);
    22              std::vector<std::string> _keys = Conversion::ListToVector(keys);
    23
    24              const auto _results = Stats::GetDescriptiveStatistics(_data, _keys);
    25              Dictionary<String^, double>^ results = Conversion::ResultsToDictionary(_results);
    26              return results;
    27              STATS_CATCH
    28          }
    29    ⊞     // ...
    32    □     Dictionary<String^, double>^ Statistics::DescriptiveStatistics(List<double>^ data)
    33          {
    34              return DescriptiveStatistics(data, nullptr);
    35          }
```

In Listing 3-2, the function begins by converting the incoming managed `List<double>` to a `std::vector<double>`. Similarly the keys are converted from `List<String^>` to `std::vector<std::string>`. Following this, we pass the parameters to our native function and it returns the results packaged as a `std::unordered_map` with a `string` as the key and a `double` value. The results package is then converted back to a managed dictionary and passed back to the caller. We will deal with the conversions in some more detail in the following. Local variables are declared with a leading underscore to distinguish them from the parameters and return values. This just avoids coming up with additional variable names.

The native C++ function `GetDescriptiveStatistics` has a default second parameter, the vector of keys. Users of the function are given a choice of being able to supply keys in order to request specific results, or supply a single parameter in order to get back all the results. To represent this in C++/CLI, we need to provide an overloaded version of the function with a single parameter. This is also shown in Listing 3-2. The code in the single parameter overload forwards the call to the full version, supplying a `nullptr` as the second parameter. This will allow the client to call either the single parameter version or the two-parameter version of the function.

Linear Regression

The implementation of the `LinearRegression` wrapper follows a similar structure to `DescriptiveStatistics`. Listing 3-3 shows the code.

Listing 3-3. The implementation of the `LinearRegression` wrapper function

```
Statistics.cpp    ⇥ ×   Statistics.h
StatsCLR                          ▼ ⇨ StatsCLR::Statistics                         ▼ ◉ LinearRegression(List<double>^ xs, List<double>^ ys)
    36
    37          // ...
    40          Dictionary<String^, double>^ Statistics::LinearRegression(List<double>^ xs, List<double>^ ys)
    41          {
    42              STATS_TRY
    43                  const auto _xs = Conversion::ListToVector(xs);
    44                  const auto _ys = Conversion::ListToVector(ys);
    45
    46                  const auto _results = Stats::LinearRegression(_xs, _ys);
    47                  const auto results = Conversion::ResultsToDictionary(_results);
    48                  return results;
    49              STATS_CATCH
    50          }
    51      }
```

In the case of the `LinearRegression` function, there are two datasets. So, we perform the conversion to a `std::vector<double>` for each dataset. Following this, we call the native C++ `LinearRegression` function and get the results package. These are then converted to the managed type we have chosen, in this case a `Dictionary`. Note that we can use the keyword `auto` for both native C++ and managed code. In general terms, writing C++/CLI code is practically identical to writing native C++ code.

Type Conversion

Now that we have seen the basic statistics functions `DescriptiveStatistics` and `LinearRegression`, we take a look at type conversions. In C++/CLI, we do not need to explicitly convert built-in types. In our code, functions that use `bool`, `double`, or `std::size_t` (or `long`) either as parameters or return values do not require explicit marshaling. In general, the built-in C++ types are aliases of the corresponding types defined in the `System` namespace. However, we do need to convert the following types: `std::string`, `std::vector<double>`, and `std::unordered_map<std::string, double>`.

In the `Conversion` namespace, we define the following two functions:

```
void MarshalString(String^ s, std::string& os)
void MarshalString(String^ s, std::wstring& os)
```

These are standard functions to marshal strings to and from a managed environment. The function `Marshal::StringToHGlobalAnsi` takes a `String^` and converts it into a null-terminated pointer to char*. The chars are then assigned to a `std::string`, and the memory that was allocated is freed by `FreeHGlobal`. An overridden version of the function handles the case of wide-character strings (UTF-16 Unicode strings on Windows).

We also define two functions to convert lists to vectors. The first `ListToVector` function converts a generic `List<double>` to a `std::vector<double>`. The second one converts a generic `List<String^>` to `std::vector<std::string>`. In principle, it is a simple matter to copy items from a managed container (`List<double>^`) and place them in an unmanaged STL container. The initial implementation is shown in Listing 3-4.

Listing 3-4. Converting `List<double>` to `std::vector<double>`

```
Conversion.cpp  ⊕ ✕  Conversion.h
StatsCLR                    ▾  {} StatsCLR::Conversion                          ▾  ● ListToVector(List<double>^ input)
37  ⊞        // ...
40  ⊟        std::vector<double> ListToVector(List<double>^ input)
41          {
42              std::vector<double> output;
43  ⊟          if(input != nullptr)
44              {
45                  const int count = input->Count;
46                  output.resize(count);
47                  for (int i = 0; i < count; ++i)
48                      output[i] = input[i];   // native double <--> system.double
49              }
50              return output;
51          }
```

The first thing we do is to construct an empty output vector. After we check the input pointer, we obtain a count of the input items and use this to size the `std::vector<double>`. We then extract each item from the input list and place it in the output vector. The `ListToVector` override for strings follows similar logic, but uses `MarshalString` to explicitly convert from managed strings to `std::string`. It is worth emphasizing that in both these cases, we are taking entities from managed memory (doubles, strings) and copying them into unmanaged C++ memory.

In terms of performance, doing an elementwise copy is unlikely to be the most performant approach. There are various ways to improve on this. One possibility is to take advantage of "pinning." In normal circumstances, the CLR manages the memory associated with objects. Among other things, this means that it is free to move memory around. However, in certain circumstances, it might be desirable to be able to tell the

CLR not to move some memory temporarily. This is what pinning achieves. The `pin_ptr<T>` type allows you to indicate to the CLR that the memory should not be moved until the pinning pointer goes out of scope. Listing 3-5 demonstrates this approach by copying a `cli::array` to a `std::vector` using `std::copy`.

Listing 3-5. Pinning a CLI array

```
Conversion.cpp  ☐ ✕  Conversion.h
StatsCLR                    ▾  {} StatsCLR::Conversion                     ▾  ArrayToVector(cli::array<double>^ input)
    72
    73          std::vector<double> ArrayToVector(cli::array<double>^ input)
    74          {
    75              const std::size_t count = input->Length;
    76              std::vector<double> output(count);
    77              pin_ptr<double> pin(&input[0]);
    78              double* first(pin);
    79              double* last(pin + count);
    80              std::copy(first, last, output.begin());
    81              return output;
    82          }
```

In this example, we obtain a count of the input items and use this to size the `std::vector<double>`, as previously. Then we create a pinned pointer to the `cli::array` and obtain pointers to the `first` and `last` elements. The purpose of the `pin_ptr` is to ensure that the GC does not move or delete the memory during the copy operation. Finally we use `std::copy` to copy the block of memory.

Our intention in changing from using `ListToVector` to using `ArrayToVector` was to improve the performance. However, in order to do this, we have needed to change the input type from `List<double>` to `cli::array<double>`. We have also needed to change the function call to:

```
static Dictionary<String^, double>^ DescriptiveStatistics(cli::array<double>^ data);
```

And lastly, we have needed to change the call to the type conversion code to use `ArrayToVector` instead of `ListToVector`. As we said previously, there are choices to be made in the conversion layer.

The second conversion function converts a `std::unordered_map` to a `Dictionary`. Listing 3-6 shows the code.

Listing 3-6. Converting the results package to a `Dictionary`

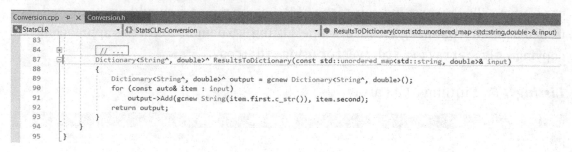

```
// ...
Dictionary<String^, double>^ ResultsToDictionary(const std::unordered_map<std::string, double>& input)
{
    Dictionary<String^, double>^ output = gcnew Dictionary<String^, double>();
    for (const auto& item : input)
        output->Add(gcnew String(item.first.c_str()), item.second);
    return output;
}
```

The conversion from the results packaged in a `std::unordered_map` to a `Dictionary` is working in the opposite direction from the previous conversion functions. We instantiate a new managed `Dictionary` using gcnew. This returns us a garbage collected reference. Then we iteratively place the items from the unmanaged container (input) into the managed container (output). The `Add` method takes two parameters corresponding to the `Dictionary` key-value pair. The key is a managed `string` and therefore we need to convert the `std::string` key to a `System::String` instance. Again, we use gcnew. The managed `String` class has a constructor that takes a pointer to a native array of `chars`. As before, we are performing the marshalling task manually.

The conversion functions we have used earlier are completely specific to handling the types used in StatsLib. However, there are a number of ways that this could be made more general. For example, it could be useful to generalize the `ArrayToVector` conversion (Listing 3-5) to work for any `array<T>` to `vector<T>`. Or we might prefer to convert between `std::array<T>` and `cli::array<T>`. We could also make use of the facilities provided by the `cliext` namespace. A different possibility involves using the C++ Interop. One final alternative that is worth mentioning (but which we have not pursued here) is to roll-your-own C++ "object-with-type-information." If all the C++ types can be wrapped in a common entity alongside type information (e.g., the COM `VARIANT` class), then we can, with some work, define standard conversions from/to those types to/from `System::Object` (the base class of all .NET types). This has the advantage that callers don't need to choose the types they convert to/from. In order to do this, you would need to write a C++ class that can handle converting both built-in types as well as composite types and containers. This is not a completely trivial undertaking. This type of approach is used in other frameworks. Rcpp, for example, uses `RObject*` and CPython uses `PyObject*` to wrap up native C++ types. We will see examples of these in later chapters. This approach gives you full control both over how the type conversions are done, and also full control over the set of allowable conversions. However, this is probably only appropriate if you have a lot of type conversion logic. The main point of all of this is to give you a sense of how flexible the conversion layer can be.

Exception Handling

Because this is a translation layer, we need to be aware of exceptions. Specifically, we want to ensure that exceptions thrown from the unmanaged C++ layer are handled in our code and not propagated in an untranslated form to the clients using our wrapper component. For this reason, we wrap each function call with the macros STATS_TRY/ STATS_CATCH. Listing 3-7 shows the definitions of the macros.

Listing 3-7. Exception handling in the managed wrapper

```
pch.h + X
StatsCLR                    ▼    (Global Scope)                          ▼
    10
    11      #define STATS_TRY try{
    12
    13      #define STATS_CATCH \
    14          }catch(const std::exception& e){  \
    15              System::String^ s = gcnew System::String(e.what());\
    16              System::InvalidOperationException^ se = gcnew System::InvalidOperationException(s);\
    17              throw se;  \
    18          }
```

The code catches any std::exception and creates a new managed exception of type InvalidOperationException, passing it the original exception string (appropriately converted). C# clients will therefore be able to view and handle these exceptions. Clearly, this could be generalized. The Standard Library defines many more types of exceptions, and it might be useful to translate these into more appropriately managed exception types.

Testing the Code
StatsCLR.UnitTests

With this in place, we can build and test the library. For testing the StatsCLR component, we use a C# MSUnitTest project called StatsCLR.UnitTests. It references the StatsCLR project and provides a simple means to test the functionality. To keep things simple, we only have a single file, *UnitTests.cs*. This contains test cases for `DescriptiveStatistics` and for `LinearRegression` as well as tests for the statistical hypothesis testing functionality and the `DataManager` class. This is similar to the approach we used in the native C++ (GoogleTest) unit tests we wrote for the underlying StatsLib. A typical test method is shown in Listing 3-8.

Listing 3-8. Testing the `LinearRegression` function

```
UnitTests.cs    ⊐  ✕
StatsCLR.UnitTests                  StatsCLR.UnitTests.UnitTests                          TestLinearRegression()
    38
    39                      [TestMethod]
    40                      public void TestLinearRegression()
    41                      {
    42                          // Arrange
    43                          List<double> xs = new List<double> { 0, 1, 2, 3, 4, 5, 6, 7, 8, 9 };
    44                          List<double> ys = new List<double> { 1, 3, 2, 5, 7, 8, 8, 9, 10, 12 };
    45
    46                          // Act
    47                          Dictionary<string, double> results = Statistics.LinearRegression(xs, ys);
    48
    49                          // Assert
    50                          Assert.AreEqual(1.2363636, results["b0"], 1e-6);
    51                          Assert.AreEqual(1.1696969, results["b1"], 1e-6);
    52                      }
```

The test function uses the attribute `[TestMethod]`. This means we can run it from the Test menu in Visual Studio (and from the Test Explorer panel). As previously, the test follows the *arrange-act-assert* pattern.[3] We supply the data in the expected form and call the `LinearRegression` function. The results are then compared to expected values. In addition, we test that the function throws the expected exception when called with empty data. Listing 3-9 shows the code for this.

---

[3] The *arrange-act-assert* pattern is described in more detail here: https://docs.microsoft.com/en-us/visualstudio/test/unit-test-basics?view=vs-2019.

Listing 3-9. Testing exception handling

```
UnitTests.cs  -¤  X
StatsCLR.UnitTests                    ▾  StatsCLR.UnitTests.UnitTests                              ▾  TestDescriptiveStatisticsThrows()
    53
    54              [TestMethod]
    55              [ExpectedException(typeof(InvalidOperationException))]
    56  ⌐          public void TestDescriptiveStatisticsThrows()
    57              {
    58                  // Arrange
    59                  List<double> xs = new List<double>();
    60                  List<string> keys = new List<string>();
    61
    62                  // Act
    63                  Dictionary<string, double> results = Statistics.DescriptiveStatistics(xs, keys);
    64              }
```

As before, we attribute this as a [TestMethod]. In addition, we declare the
[ExpectedException] attribute parameterized with the exception type we are
expecting. In the function body, we declare an empty list and pass this to the
DescriptiveStatistics function. The exception is thrown in the underlying C++
layer and not in the conversion function. Similarly, if we pass in a null reference, the
conversion function passes an empty std::vector<double> to the underlying C++
function, which throws the corresponding exception. As an alternative to using the
[ExpectedException] attribute, we could write the following in the preceding // Act
section:

```
Assert.ThrowsException<InvalidOperationException>(() => Statistics.
DescriptiveStatistics(xs));
```

This achieves the same result as using the attribute.

Managed Wrapper Classes

Introduction

So far, we have written code to wrap the native C++ functions. We have also converted
to and from the Standard Library types. However, there is still some ground to cover in
order to expose the rest of the functionality from StatsLib. We still want the functionality
offered by the DataManager and the statistical test classes.

To make this functionality available, we need to write a managed wrapper class around an unmanaged object. This approach is quite straightforward. We define a managed class that contains a private member variable that points to the underlying unmanaged C++ type. Then, we use the constructor to create a new instance of this unmanaged type using `operator new`. For each underlying function we want to expose, we declare an equivalent managed member function that forwards the call to the underlying type. The function takes care of converting arguments to the appropriate underlying types. When the managed object is being disposed of, we delete the pointer to the underlying C++ type. This approach is similar to the "pointer-to-implementation" (*pimpl*) design pattern. We have distinct classes that separate the (managed) interface from the (unmanaged) implementation details.

The DataManager

The `DataManager` is a typical wrapper class. It follows the *pimpl* idiom as shown in Listing 3-10.

Listing 3-10. The DataManager wrapper class

```
DataManager.h  ⊉ ✕
StatsCLR                    ▾    StatsCLR::DataManager                    ▾    DataManager()
     8
     9     ⊟namespace StatsCLR
    10      {
    11          // The DataManager manages named data sets.
    12     ⊟    public ref class DataManager
    13          {
    14          public:
    15              // Constructor
    16              DataManager();
    17
    18              // Finalizer
    19              !DataManager();
    20
    21              // Destruction
    22              ~DataManager();
    23
    24              // Count the number of data sets currently held by the DataManager
    25              unsigned long long CountDataSets();
    26
    27              // Add a named data set to the DataManager collection
    28              bool Add(String^ name, List<double>^ vals);
    29
    30              // Retrieve a named data set from the DataManager
    31              List<double>^ GetDataSet(String^ name);
    32
    33              // Retrieve a list of all the data sets currently in the DataManager
    34              List<Tuple<String^, unsigned long long>^>^ ListDataSets();
    35
    36              // Clear the data sets from the DataManager
    37              void ClearDataSets();
    38
    39          private:
    40              // Native pointer to the underlying C++ class
    41              Stats::DataManager* m_manager;
    42          };
    43      }
```

The DataManager wrapper class exposes all the caching functionality of the native C++ class. We can see from the class declaration that, broadly speaking, we are dealing with two aspects. Firstly, we are managing the lifetime of the native pointer Stats::DataManager*. We use the constructor and destructor to do this. Listing 3-11 shows the code.

Listing 3-11. Instantiating the native pointer in our wrapper class

```
DataManager.cpp  ⊕ ✕  DataManager.h
StatsCLR                      ▼ ⇨ StatsCLR::DataManager                        ▼ ● DataManager()
    12  ⊞       // ...
    15  ⊟       DataManager::DataManager()
    16           {
    17               STATS_TRY
    18               m_manager = new Stats::DataManager();
    19               STATS_CATCH
    20           }
```

The constructor follows the semantics of the underlying class. In this case, there are no arguments to pass so we simply create a new instance. The destructor behaves in a similar way to a native C++ destructor. It is deterministic, so when the object goes out of scope the destructor is called. In addition, there is a non-deterministic finalizer that is called by the GC. The code for both types of destructors are shown in Listing 3-12.

Listing 3-12. The DataManager destructors

```
DataManager.cpp  ⊕ ✕  DataManager.h
StatsCLR                      ▼ ⇨ StatsCLR::DataManager                        ▼ ● ~DataManager()
    21  ⊟       //
    22           // Destructor
    23           //
    24  ⊟       DataManager::~DataManager()
    25           {
    26               this->!DataManager();
    27           }
    28
    29  ⊟       //
    30           // Finalizer
    31           //
    32  ⊟       DataManager::!DataManager()
    33           {
    34               delete m_manager;
    35           }
```

From Listing 3-12, we can see that in the finalizer, we explicitly call the destructor. Destructors in a C++/CLI reference type perform deterministic clean-up of resources. Finalizers clean up unmanaged resources and can be called deterministically by the destructor (as we do in this case) or non-deterministically by the garbage collector. What is important here is that the unmanaged memory of the implementation class is explicitly released via the destructor. If not, a memory leak will occur.

In addition to lifetime management, the second thing we are doing in the DataManager is to forward calls to the underlying object and to return results. Specifically, we need to forward calls to retrieve a count of the datasets, to add a new dataset, to retrieve a named dataset, to list all the datasets with a count of items, and finally, to clear all the datasets. Listing 3-13 shows the function GetDataSet.

Listing 3-13. The implementation of the GetDataSet function

```
DataManager.cpp  ⊕ ✕  DataManager.h
StatsCLR                      ▼  ⇨ StatsCLR::DataManager              ▼  ● GetDataSet(String ^ name)
  68    ⊞        // ...
  71    ⊟        List<double>^ DataManager::GetDataSet(String^ name)
  72             {
  73                 STATS_TRY
  74
  75                 std::string _name;
  76                 Conversion::MarshalString(name, _name);
  77
  78                 std::vector<double> _data = m_manager->GetDataSet(_name);
  79
  80                 List<double>^ data = gcnew List<double>();
  81                 for (const double d : _data)
  82                     data->Add(d);
  83                 return data;
  84
  85                 STATS_CATCH
  86             }
```

The GetDataSet function retrieves a named dataset from the native DataManager class. Prior to calling the function, we convert the name parameter to a std::string. The dataset is returned as a vector of doubles. Therefore, when we return the result, we explicitly convert it to a List. All the time, we need to be aware that we are acting as a boundary between the managed and the unmanaged world. Therefore, we need to convert incoming parameters to native types and when we get returned native types, we need to convert them to managed types.

The TTest Class

The TTtest class is similar to the DataManager. In this case, we have chosen not to expose the base class (StatisticalTest). We could have recreated the hierarchy in the managed context; however, it is not necessary, so we limit ourselves to just exposing the TTest class. Listing 3-14 shows the complete class declaration.

Listing 3-14. Class declaration for the TTest

```
StatisticalTests.h  ⊟  ✕
StatsCLR                        ▼  StatsCLR::TTest                          ▼
   11    ⊟     public ref class TTest
   12          {
   13          public:
   14              // Constructors
   15
   16              // Summary data: population mean, sample mean, sample standard deviation, sample size.
   17              TTest(double mu0, double x_bar, double sx, double n);
   18
   19              // One-sample: population mean, sample.
   20              TTest(double mu0, List<double>^ x1);
   21
   22              // Two-sample
   23              TTest(List<double>^ x1, List<double>^ x2);
   24
   25              // Finalizer
   26              !TTest();
   27
   28              // Destructor
   29              ~TTest();
   30
   31              // Perform the test
   32              bool Perform();
   33
   34              // Retrieve the results
   35              Dictionary<String^, double>^ Results();
   36
   37          private:
   38              // Native pointer to the underlying C++ class
   39              Stats::TTest* m_test;
   40          };
```

As before, we wrap a native pointer `Stats::TTest*` in a managed class. In this case, we mimic the construction semantics of the native class. Each constructor instantiates the appropriate native pointer type using the parameters it is passed. For example, the constructor for the one-sample t-test is shown in Listing 3-15.

Listing 3-15. The `TTest` constructor for a one-sample t-test

```
StatisticalTests.cpp  ⊞ ×   StatisticalTests.h
StatsCLR                 ▼    (Global Scope)                                    ▼
    23    │
    24  ⊞ │    // ...
    27  ⊟ │    TTest::TTest(double mu0, List<double>^ x1)
    28    │    {
    29    │        STATS_TRY
    30    │
    31    │        std::vector<double> _x1 = Conversion::ListToVector(x1);
    32    │        m_test = new Stats::TTest(mu0, _x1);
    33    │
    34    │        STATS_CATCH
    35    │    }
```

In the case of a one-sample t-test, we pass in a `double` and a `List<double>`. The first parameter is implicitly converted, while we convert the second explicitly using our conversion function `ListToVector`. Finally, we create a new unmanaged `TTest` object, handling any exceptions that might be thrown.

As we can see, even with these simple examples, being able to expose user-defined types to clients, rather than writing procedural wrapper functions, provides a richer way to interoperate with native C++ code. We are able to more accurately reflect the semantics of the underlying C++ types, while at the same time allowing us freedom of choice over what is exposed.

It is worth emphasizing what we have accomplished in relatively few lines of code. We have exposed all the functionality from a C++ library in a fully working wrapper component that can be used in the .NET framework. Developing this component is quite straightforward, especially when considered in comparison with writing an equivalent COM wrapper.

A COM wrapper built, for example, using ATL/COM requires more infrastructure. At a minimum, the interfaces and implementations need to be registered. Exposing functions and classes, while not difficult, is more involved than working with the C++/CLI. We would need to create new COM interfaces (`IStatisticalTest, IDataManager,` for example) that would be implemented in an ATL/COM class. This class would also provide implementations of other standard interfaces (`IDispatch` and `IErrorInfo,` for example). While a good deal of this code is boilerplate and generated for us, it is still more complex than working with a C++/CLI `ref class`. Furthermore, for functions that do not use built-in types, we would need to deal with conversions to and from a VARIANT. These are not completely trivial. Consider, for example, the case of converting a std::unordered_map<std::string, double> into a SafeArray attached to a VARIANT. The StatsATLCOM project illustrates some of these issues.[4] Overall, the C++/CLI wrapper provides a simpler alternative while allowing us to develop code using native C++.

Summary

In this chapter, we have built a C++/CLI wrapper around the StatsLib. We have used this wrapper to expose both functions and classes while converting types where required. We have also seen a simple example of how a C# client can consume this functionality in the unit test project. In the next chapter, we have a look at a more complex scenario using Excel as a client.

In such a small space there is clearly a lot we haven't covered. We haven't touched on delegates and events. These are important if you need to use callbacks from a native C++ environment. We have mentioned "pinning," but not covered "boxing," as we are trying to keep things simple. There are numerous small details relating to the niceties of memory management in both the managed and unmanaged worlds that we haven't covered. The Additional Resources section and the References provide links to documents that cover the topics in more detail.

Overall, using C++/CLI is extremely useful if you have to migrate existing code to the .NET platform. By writing a wrapper component, we have added a layer of indirection which helps when it comes to refactoring the underlying code. As pointed out in Chapter 2, we could have written a COM wrapper around the StatsLib (also maintaining the separation of concerns), and then used the facilities provided by the COM Interop to directly use the component in a .NET project. However, as we noted earlier, this is likely to require more infrastructure, and lead to a more complex architecture than using C++/CLI.

---

[4] The StatsATLCOM project simply mirrors part of the functionality of the StatsCLR wrapper. Its purpose is to illustrate some of the differences and difficulties involved in writing COM wrappers as opposed to using C++/CLI as an approach for connecting C++ to C# and .NET.

Additional Resources

The following links provide more detailed information on the topics covered in this chapter:

- The C++/CLI Language Specification provides the most comprehensive reference document covering all the language features. It can be downloaded from here: `www.ecma-international.org/publications-and-standards/standards/ecma-372/`.

- If you need some additional information about the C++/CLI language, the Microsoft documentation ".NET programming with C++/CLI" is a good place to start: `https://docs.microsoft.com/en-us/cpp/dotnet/dotnet-programming-with-cpp-cli-visual-cpp?view=msvc-160`.

- For a discussion about the rationale for C++/CLI, there is a useful article by Herb Sutter at `www.gotw.ca/publications/C++CLIRationale.pdf`.

- For more information about mixing native and managed assemblies, the following documentation is useful: `https://docs.microsoft.com/en-us/cpp/dotnet/mixed-native-and-managed-assemblies?view=msvc-160`.

- The `cliext` namespace contains all the types of the STL/CLR library. This is described here: `https://docs.microsoft.com/en-us/cpp/dotnet/stl-clr-library-reference?view=msvc-160`.

- Using the C++ Interop is described here: `https://docs.microsoft.com/en-us/cpp/dotnet/how-to-marshal-arrays-using-cpp-interop?view=msvc-160`.

- For further information on destructors and finalizers in C++/CLI, see the following: `https://docs.microsoft.com/en-us/previous-versions/visualstudio/visual-studio-2008/ms177197(v=vs.90)?redirectedfrom=MSDN`.

- Full details on "boxing" and "pinning" can be found at `https://docs.microsoft.com/en-us/cpp/dotnet/boxing-cpp-cli?view=msvc-160` and `https://docs.microsoft.com/en-us/cpp/extensions/pin-ptr-cpp-cli?view=msvc-160`.

Exercises

The exercises in this section provide some hands-on practice in making native C++ functionality available to .NET clients via a C++/CLI wrapper component.

There are three main changes we made to the C++ layer that we are interested in exposing:

- We added more results to the `LinearRegression` function.

- We added a `ZTest` class which performs statistical z-tests. This is similar to the `TTest` class so we can base any new code on this.

- We added a `TimeSeries` class with a function to calculate a simple moving average.

1) In the StatsCLR.UnitTests project, extend the test method `TestLinearRegression` to incorporate tests for the correlation coefficient r and the r^2 measure. Rebuild and rerun the tests and confirm there are no errors.

2) In the StatsCLR project, expose the z-test functionality. While it would be perfectly possible to add procedural wrappers for the `ZTest` functionality to the *Statistics.h* and *Statistics.cpp*, it is preferable to create a managed `ZTest` class that wraps the underlying native C++ class and calls the `Perform` and `Results` functions. This approach is described in the section on Managed wrapper classes.

The steps required are as follows:

- In *StatisticalTests.h*, add `public ref class ZTest { };`. Follow the class definition used for `TTest` wrapper.

- In *StatisticalTests.cpp*, add the class implementation. The constructors need to call appropriate versions of the underlying C++ constructors. Existing conversion functions can be used to convert the constructor arguments to Standard Library types. The implementation of `Perform` and `Results` simply forward the calls to the underlying unmanaged native instance. The results need to be converted to a managed `Dictionary`. Again, this can be done using the existing conversion function.

- Rebuild the StatsCLR project. In StatsCLR.UnitTests, add test cases for the three types of z-test that we deal with: `TestSummaryDataZTest`, `TestOneSampleZTest`, and `TestTwoSampleZTest`. These are similar to the test cases for the native C++ class and can use the same data. Check that the test cases run without errors.

3) Expose the `TimeSeries` class. This is similar to the previous exercise but is somewhat more involved, as we need to add a conversion function to handle the input list of dates and another conversion function to return the list of moving average values.

The steps required are as follows:

- Add the files *TimeSeries.h* and *TimeSeries.cpp* to the project.

- In the header file, add the line to include the native C++ class declaration:

  ```
  #include "..\include\TimeSeries.h"
  ```

- Add the following using declarations:

  ```
  using namespace System;
  using namespace System::Collections::Generic;
  using namespace System::Text;
  ```

- Add the class definition with appropriate C++/CLI types. In the case of the "dates," the native C++ class treats these as `long`s. While we could just have a list of `long`s, in .NET the `DateTime` class is more useful. We should be able to make use of the `.ToOADate` member function to get a serial number. The suggested `TimeSeries` constructor arguments are therefore

  ```
  List<System::DateTime>^ dates, List<double>^ observations
  ```

  The `MovingAverage` member function should return a `List<double>^`.

- In the implementation file, add

  ```
  #include "pch.h"
  #include "Conversion.h"
  #include "TimeSeries.h"
  ```

- Add the class definition (constructor, destructor, finalizer, and `MovingAverage` function). For the constructor argument `List<System::DateTime>^ dates`, we need to add a conversion function:

  ```
  std::vector<long> ListToVector(List<System::DateTime>^ dates);
  ```

- For the `MovingAverage` function, we can forward the `window` argument directly to the unmanaged class instance. However, we need to convert the returned `vector` to a `List`:

  ```
  List<double>^ VectorToList(const std::vector<double>& input);
  ```

- In the `Conversion` namespace, add the following function declarations:

  ```
  std::vector<long> ListToVector(List<System::DateTime>^ dates);
  List<double>^ VectorToList(const std::vector<double>& input);
  ```

- In the file *Conversion.cpp*, add the implementations. These are similar to the existing conversion functions.

- Rebuild the StatsCLR project. In StatsCLR.UnitTests, add a test method called `TestMovingAverage`. This will be similar to the test case for the native C++ class. Check that the test cases run without errors.

## CHAPTER 4

C# Clients: Consuming the Managed Wrapper

Introduction

In this chapter, we look at consuming StatsCLR, the C++/CLI component we have built in the previous chapter. To some extent, we have done this already with the StatsCLR. UnitTests testing module. However, in this chapter, we take a broader look at using the component in a variety of different contexts.

Our first application is a plain C# console application. When looking at how we might use a wrapper component, we have three main objectives. Firstly, we want to check that the component works correctly, and that we can call the functions and get the expected results. Therefore, initially, we just look at test-driving some of the functionality that we have exposed in a simple context. Secondly, we would like to know if we can use the component alongside other components. One of the main reasons for developing components is to leverage other .NET components. For this, we look at how the statistical functions might fit into a simple machine learning (ML) pipeline using Accord. NET. Lastly, we want to check whether the component implements the functionality available by virtue of being a .NET component. For this, we look at reflection.

Our second application is more focused on the real-world. We look at connecting our component to Excel and using the basic statistical functionality from StatsLib.

© Adam Gladstone 2022
A. Gladstone, *C++ Software Interoperability for Windows Programmers*,
https://doi.org/10.1007/978-1-4842-7966-3_4

StatsClient

Project Settings

StatsClient is built as a C# Console Application. The only setting of interest is the Platform target. Under the project properties for Build, we set the Platform target to "x64". This is consistent with the underlying StatsLib C++ library, and the StatsCLR C++/CLI component. If we don't do this, we will get a compiler warning about a mismatch between the processor architecture and the project, and more importantly, when we run the executable, the assembly will fail to load, with an obscure error message. We have also added a reference to the StatsCLR project under the project References node.

Installing Accord.NET

Accord.NET (http://accord-framework.net/) is a .NET ML framework. It has a wide variety of modules, but we limit ourselves to only using the core ML module, the Controls module, and the IO module. We have installed these into StatsClient using the package manager. The dependencies are listed in the file *packages.config*. You can check under Tools ➤ NuGet Package Manager ➤ Manage NuGet Packages for Solution... if the packages require installation or updates.

Code Organization

The code in the StatsClient project is organized into six files plus the main `Program` class. These are listed as follows with a brief description of each:

- *StatisticalFunctions.cs* exercises the descriptive statistics and linear regression functions using the `DataManager` wrapper.

- *DataAnalysis.cs* performs a simple analysis of some time series finance data.

- *DataModelling.cs* creates a simple linear data model for house prices based on a single feature, house size.

- *HypothesisTest.cs* performs a two-sample student t-test and reports the alternative hypothesis.

- *ModuleInfo.cs* demonstrates extracting module information from an assembly.

- *DynamicInvocation.cs* demonstrates both dynamic loading of an assembly and dynamic invocation of functions.

- *Program.cs* contains the main routine that calls the example code.

Statistical Functions

The code in *StatisticalFunctions.cs* runs through a typical session. We begin by creating an instance of the data manager, and we add two datasets to it, which we name 'xs' and 'ys'. After this, we retrieve the descriptive statistics for the 'xs' dataset and output the results to the console. This is shown in Figure 4-1.

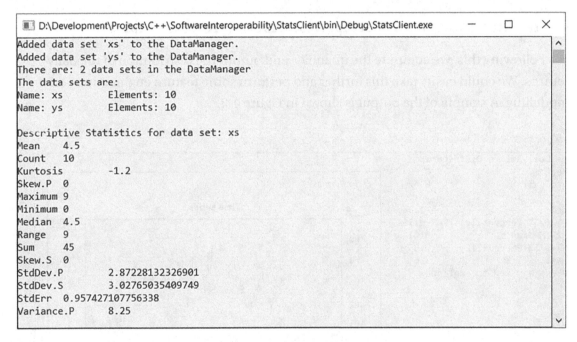

Figure 4-1. *Testing the* `DescriptiveStatistics` *function*

Next, we perform a linear regression using the same datasets that we loaded initially, and output the results. The final part of the session consists of creating an instance of the t-test class. We pass in the constructor arguments that correspond to a summary data t-test and then we call `Perform` and retrieve the results, displaying them on the console.

Data Analysis

The *DataAnalysis.cs* module combines usage of the `DescriptiveStatistics` function with additional statistical analysis functions from Accord.NET. The purpose of the routine is to analyze the distribution of the returns of the EUR/USD exchange rate from 01-Jan-1999 until 29-Dec-2017. The code begins by reading in the data for the daily EUR/USD exchange rate. After reading the data, we display the time series. Using our `DescriptiveStatistics` function, we request a number of summary measures (*Maximum, Mean, Median, Minimum, StdDev.S, Q1, Q3*) describing the returns as follows:

```
List<double> _returns = new List<double>(returns);
List<string> stats = new List<string>() { "Maximum", "Mean", "Median",
"Minimum", "StdDev.S", "Q1", "Q3" };
var results = Statistics.DescriptiveStatistics(_returns, stats);
```

Following this, we compute the quantiles and output the distribution of the daily returns. We could easily take this further and perform some feature engineering and modelling. A sample of the output is shown in Figure 4-2.

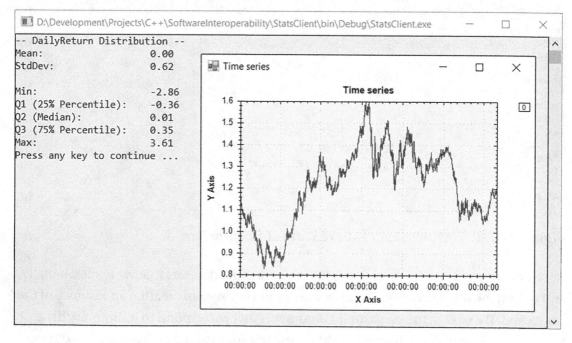

Figure 4-2. *Analyzing the distribution of returns for EUR/USD*

Data Modelling

In the module *DataModelling.cs* we use the StatsCLR component as part of an ML pipeline. The code is shown in Listing 4-1.

Listing 4-1. Modelling house prices

```
DataModelling.cs  ⊟  ✕
[C#] StatsClient                        ▾  ⚑ StatsClient.DataModelling         ▾  ⊕ Predict(double b0, double b1, double x)

26        // 1. Import or create training data
27        string filename = @"..\..\..\Data\HouseData.csv";
28        Accord.IO.CsvReader reader = new Accord.IO.CsvReader(filename, true);
29
30        System.Data.DataTable dt = reader.ToTable();
31        double[] size = dt.AsEnumerable()
32                  .Select(row => Convert.ToDouble(row.Field<string>("Size"),
33                  System.Globalization.CultureInfo.InvariantCulture)).ToArray();
34        double[] price = dt.AsEnumerable()
35                  .Select(row => Convert.ToDouble(row.Field<string>("Price"),
36                  System.Globalization.CultureInfo.InvariantCulture)).ToArray();
37
38        // 2. Specify data preparation and model training pipeline
39        List<double> ys = new List<double>(price);
40        List<double> xs = new List<double>(size);
41
42        // 3. Train model
43        var results = Statistics.LinearRegression(xs, ys);
44        double b0 = results["b0"];
45        double b1 = results["b1"];
46
47        // 4. Make a prediction
48        double new_size = 2.5;
49        var predicted_price = Predict(b0, b1, new_size);
50
51        Console.WriteLine($"(StatsCLR):\tPredicted price for size: "
52                          + $"{new_size * 1000} sq ft= {predicted_price * 100:C}k");
```

The first two stages consist of importing the training data and preparing it for input into the model. The dataset is a small set of house price data and consists of two columns: size and price. For the purposes of this model, we assume simplistically that house price is uniquely determined by a single feature: size (the floor area in square feet, to be exact). A more complex model would use more features and would attempt to determine which features had the most impact on price. Then, we fit the model using our LinearRegression function. Lastly, we extract the coefficients in order to predict the price based on a new input size. A more extensive example would have split the dataset into a training portion and a testing portion, and would use the testing portion to determine how good the model fit is. In this simple demonstration, we ignore these issues. We also compare the model with the OrdinaryLeastSquares regression model produced using Accord.NET. The results are identical as expected.

Hypothesis Testing

In the module *HypothesisTest.cs*, we perform a two-sample t-test (assuming equal variances) of the US vs. Japan petrol consumption data (*us_mpg.csv*, *jp_mpg.csv*). After reading the data and converting it into a format we can use, we perform the t-test and report the results. These are shown in Figure 4-3. Sample 1 corresponds to the US petrol consumption data and sample 2 to the Japan petrol consumption data.

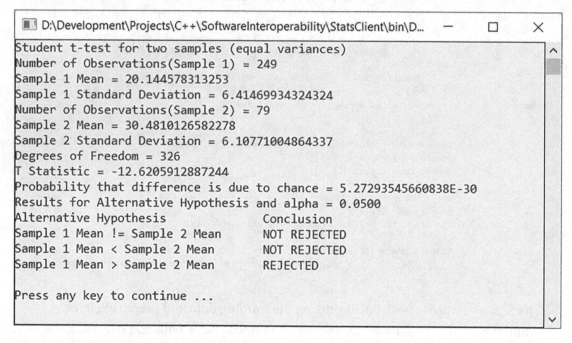

Figure 4-3. *Hypothesis test report for a two-sample t-test of US vs. Japan mpg*

As can be seen from Figure 4-3, the results indicate that the sample means are statistically significantly different. That is, cars from the United States and Japan do not typically have the same petrol consumption. In fact, the test indicates that cars from the United States have a higher petrol consumption. The probability that the difference is due to chance is extremely small. Therefore, we cannot reject the alternative hypothesis.

Apart from the ease with which we have added the StatsCLR component to our application and called the underlying C++ functions, there is nothing very surprising here. However, if we take a step back and consider that in this same application, we have dropped in other .NET components. This allows us to leverage a good deal of existing functionality. On the other hand, we could equally add a reference to StatsCLR to a different project type: perhaps a WPF application, or a web application written in ASP.NET.

Using Reflection

StatsCLR.dll is a .NET component, more specifically, an assembly. At a high level, an assembly is any .NET software component. Assemblies can be housed inside a *dll, lib,* or an *exe.* There are two main types of assemblies: private and shared. Shared assemblies require registration in the Global Assembly Cache (GAC). This topic is important in production systems but is beyond the scope of this book. In this chapter, we only deal with a single private assembly. In terms of distribution, the important point about a private assembly is that it must be located in the same directory (or sub-directory) where the executable that uses it is located.[1]

Assemblies share a number of features with traditional *dll*s, but there are important differences, particularly as regards registration and versioning. From our point of view, the most important difference is that an assembly contains metadata that describes the types and functions it contains, and that this is readily available. Assemblies can be explored using tools (e.g., the intermediate language disassembler tool *ildasm.exe*) or programmatically.

As we have said, an assembly contains metadata, compiled code, and resources. We can inspect this metadata using reflection. The .NET framework provides an API that allows us to enumerate the modules in an assembly and the types in a module. We can also enumerate the methods, fields, properties, events, and constructors for a given type, and the parameters of a method. Furthermore, we can dynamically load an assembly, create an object, and call a method at runtime. In this section, we demonstrate both of these facilities.

---

[1] The reality, as always, is more complicated. See the Additional Resources section for further information on how the .NET runtime locates assemblies.

Module Information

The code in *ModuleInfo.cs* demonstrates obtaining type information from an assembly. This could either be the current assembly or an assembly that we have explicitly loaded. The class ModuleInfo has a single function, Enumerate, that outputs to the console details of the main executable or the named assembly. This is shown in Listing 4-2.

Listing 4-2. Exploring type information in an assembly

```
ModuleInfo.cs  ⊣  ×
C# StatsClient              ▾   ◆ StatsClient.ModuleInfo          ▾  ◉ Enumerate(string assemblyName = "")
  32
  33              Console.WriteLine("Assembly Name: " + assembly.FullName);
  34              Console.WriteLine("Assembly Location: " + assembly.Location);
  35
  36              Module[] modules = assembly.GetModules();
  37              foreach (Module module in modules)
  38              {
  39                  Console.WriteLine("Module Name: " + module.FullyQualifiedName);
  40                  Type[] types = module.GetTypes();
  41                  foreach (Type type in types)
  42                  {
  43                      Console.WriteLine("\nType Name: " + type.FullName);
  44                      Console.WriteLine("Methods");
  45                      MethodInfo[] methods = type.GetMethods();
  46                      string functionString;
  47                      foreach (MethodInfo method in methods)
  48                      {
  49                          StringBuilder sbParams = new StringBuilder();
  50                          ParameterInfo[] parameters = method.GetParameters();
  51                          int paramCount = 0;
  52                          foreach (ParameterInfo parameter in parameters)
  53                          {
  54                              if (paramCount > 0 && paramCount < parameters.Length)
  55                                  sbParams.Append(", ");
  56                              sbParams.AppendFormat($"{parameter.ParameterType} {parameter.Name}");
  57                              paramCount++;
  58                          }
  59
  60                          functionString = string.Format($"\t{method.Name}({sbParams.ToString()})");
  61                          Console.WriteLine(functionString);
  62                      }
  63                  }
  64              }
```

Once we have a reference to an assembly, we can obtain a list of modules. Then, for each module, we list the types it supports, and the methods. The preceding code builds a functionString containing the function name and the parameters of each method. A quick look at the watch window when debugging shows that there is a rich description of the module. This is shown in Figure 4-4.

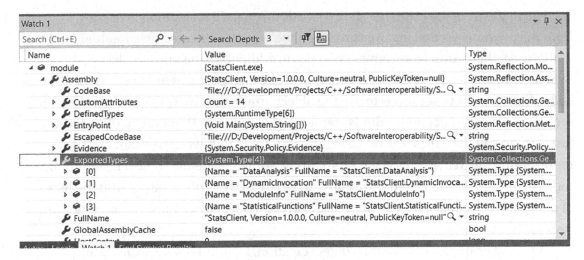

Figure 4-4. *Exported types in the watch window*

In this case, we can see the classes that we have declared in this project. We could go further and expand the exported types to discover the methods and their arguments.

Dynamic Invocation

Next, the code in *DynamicInvocation.cs*, Listing 4-3, shows both dynamic object invocation and dynamic object creation.

Listing 4-3. Invoking the `LinearRegression` function dynamically

```
DynamicInvocation.cs  ⊣ ×
StatsClient                    ▾  StatsClient.DynamicInvocation          ▾  Run()
    24                          {
    25                              // Dynamic invocation
    26                              Type type = typeof(StatsCLR.Statistics);
    27                              MethodInfo method = type.GetMethod("LinearRegression");
    28
    29                              object[] parameters = new object[2];
    30                              parameters[0] = new List<double> { 0, 1, 2, 3, 4, 5, 6, 7, 8, 9 };
    31                              parameters[1] = new List<double> { 1, 3, 2, 5, 7, 8, 8, 9, 10, 12 };
    32
    33                              object obj = new object();
    34                              object retVal = method.Invoke(obj, parameters);
    35                              Dictionary<string, double> results = (Dictionary<string, double>)retVal;
    36                              StatisticalFunctions.OutputResults(results);
    37                          }
```

The first part of the code (not shown) loads the StatsCLR assembly. We know from the previous section that we can obtain the types via the assembly module. In this case, there are a large number of types in addition to the ones we declared in StatsCLR. This is because the types include the STL types used in the C++/CLI code. A useful way to see this is to use the object browser. As we saw in the previous section, we can inspect the methods, parameters, and fields. However, in this case, we just want to call the `LinearRegression` function. To do this, we first obtain the `Type` representing the `Statistics` class. From this, we obtain a method object representing the `LinearRegression` method. We construct a `parameters` object array with the lists of data. Lastly, we make the call to `method.Invoke`. As usual, we retrieve the results and display them.

Our final example is of dynamic object creation. Listing 4-4 shows the code.

Listing 4-4. Creating an object dynamically

```
DynamicInvocation.cs ⊕ ✕
StatsClient                          StatsClient.DynamicInvocation              Run()
    39   ┌─ :          {
    40   │              // Dynamic object creation
    41   │              object[] parameters = new object[4];
    42   │              parameters[0] = 5;              // mu0
    43   │              parameters[1] = 9.261460;       // x_bar
    44   │              parameters[2] = 0.2278881e-01;  // sx;
    45   │              parameters[3] = 195;            // n
    46   │
    47   │              Type type = typeof(StatsCLR.TTest);
    48   │              TTest ttest = Activator.CreateInstance(type, parameters) as TTest;
    49   │              ttest.Perform();
    50   │              Dictionary<string, double> results = ttest.Results();
    51   │              StatisticalFunctions.OutputResults(results);
    52   └─          }
```

We start off setting up an array of input parameters corresponding to the summary data t-test. Then we obtain the type corresponding to the `TTest` class from the StatsCLR assembly. With this information, we can create an instance of the `TTest` class. For this, we use the `Activator.CreateInstance` function. This dynamically creates an instance of a `TTest` class. The parameters determine which underlying constructor is called. After performing the t-test, we retrieve the results and display them.

PowerShell

If all this seems slightly artificial, we can use PowerShell to demonstrate a more realistic example. Listing 4-5 shows a simple PowerShell script that exercises some of the functionality in StatsCLR in order to analyze the system performance counters.

Listing 4-5. Using StatsCLR to analyse performance counters

```
StatsService.ps1 ×
1  $Stats =[Reflection.Assembly]::LoadFile("D:\Development\Projects\C++\SoftwareInteroperability\x64\Debug\StatsCLR.dll")
2  $Stats.ExportedTypes
3  $data = New-Object Collections.Generic.List[double]
4  $data = (Get-Counter -counter "\Memory\% Committed Bytes In Use" -MaxSamples 10 -SampleInterval 1).CounterSamples.CookedValue
5  $keys = @("Mean", "StdDev.S", "Minimum", "Maximum")
6  [StatsCLR.Statistics]::DescriptiveStatistics($data, $keys) | Format-Table
7  [StatsCLR.Statistics]::DescriptiveStatistics($data, $keys) | Out-GridView
```

Initially, the script loads the StatsCLR assembly (just as we did previously). We display the types available for informational purposes. Next, we declare an array of doubles (using the C# `Collections.Generic.List` type). This holds the results of the call to get the performance counter named *"Memory% Committed Bytes In Use"*. We use the *CmdLet* named `Get-Counter` to retrieve data about the specified counter. For this counter, we request ten samples only, with an interval of 1 second between observations. We then set up the keys for the statistics we want (*Mean, StdDev.S, Minimum,* and *Maximum*) and make the call to `DescriptiveStatistics`. The output can be formatted in a variety of ways, and can also be piped to other *CmdLets*. In this case, we choose to output a tabular display to the console and also output the table to the default grid view. This is shown in Figure 4-5.

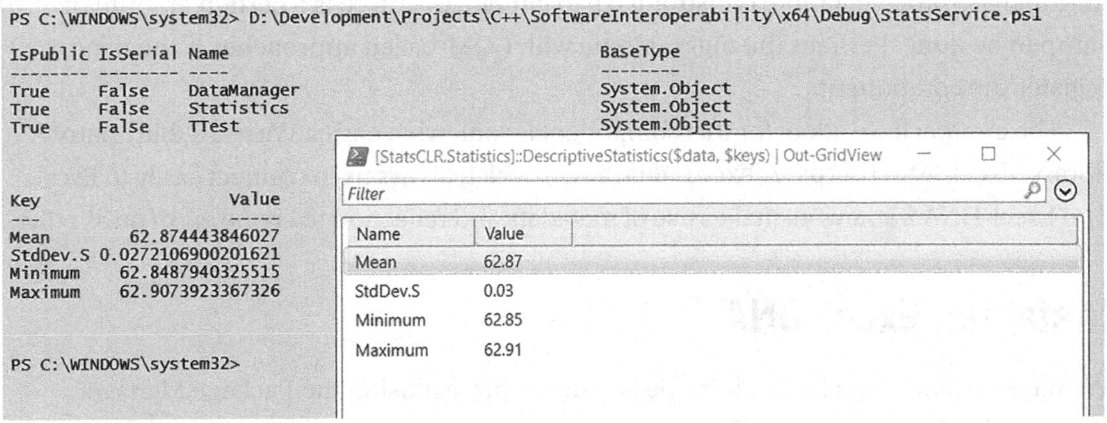

Figure 4-5. *PowerShell display of the performance counter data*

In this section, we have only scratched the surface of what can be accomplished with reflection: if we can load assemblies dynamically, then we can decide at execution time which version of an assembly to use. Alternatively, we can associate different assemblies with the implementation of interfaces and hence load different implementations on demand, for example. More generally, in terms of software design, these facilities (dynamic loading and dynamic method invocation) enable the development of systems of loosely coupled, reusable, software components which helps software interoperability.

StatsExcel

Our second C# client is somewhat more involved, and certainly more realistic than the examples in the previous section. Our goal is to be able to use the functionality provided by StatsLib in Excel. More concretely, we would like to be able to call a function in an Excel worksheet like this: `=StatisticalFunctions.LinearRegression(xs, ys)`.

Having Excel use C/C++ components has been available for a long time. And over this period, there have been a number of slightly different ways to accomplish this. One typical approach is building an *xll* by hand. An *xll* is a C/C++ *dll* housing with some additional exported functions that the Excel API defines. In particular, Excel will call the function `xlAutoOpen` when the XLL is added to Excel. The `xlAutoOpen` routine then registers each function to Excel. Once registered, the functions appear in Excel's function list. An alternative to writing an *xll* is to use a COM add-in (this could be either an Office extension add-in, which is quite flexible, or a VSTO (Visual Studio Tools for Office) add-in, which is somewhat more constrained). In either case, there is a certain amount of setup to be done. Perhaps the biggest issue with COM-based approaches is the need to register the component.

The approach we adopt for this component is somewhat easier. We use a third-party library, Excel-DNA (`https://excel-dna.net/`), which allows us to connect easily to Excel. The Excel-DNA framework makes use of metadata and reflection to create an *xll* on-the-fly.

Installing Excel-DNA

We have installed Excel-DNA into the StatsExcel project using the Package Manager. You can check under Tools ➤ NuGet Package Manager ➤ Manage NuGet Packages for Solution... if the packages require installation or updates. The Excel-DNA NuGet Package installs the required files and configures the project to build an Excel-DNA add-in.

Project Settings

The StatsExcel component is built as a C# class library. In the project properties, check that the external program is correctly referencing Excel. The setting "Start external program" should be set to point to Excel, for example, *C:\Program Files\Microsoft Office\root\Office16\EXCEL.EXE*. In addition, you can check that the command line arguments reference the x64 target we want to build: *"StatsExcel-AddIn64.xll"*.

Exposing Functions to Excel

In order to make the functions from the StatsCLR component available, we need to write additional wrapper functions and declare them as `public static` functions. When the component is built, these functions are exported to Excel and appear in the list of available functions, as shown in Figure 4-6.

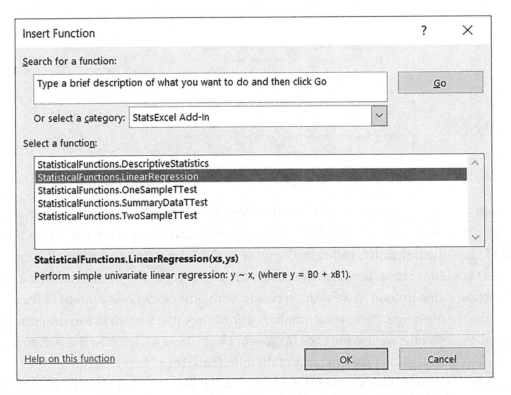

Figure 4-6. Statistical functions exposed from StatsCLR via Excel-DNA

From Figure 4-6, we can see the `DescriptiveStatistics`, `LinearRegression`, and statistical test functions listed. We can also see the *helpstring* describing the selected function. In the file *StatisticalFunctions.cs*, we declare a class that wraps up the functions we want to use. We wrap up `DescriptiveStatistics`, `LinearRegression`, and the `TTest` class just to keep things manageable. Listing 4-6 shows the `DescriptiveStatistics` function.

Listing 4-6. The `DescriptiveStatistics` function

```
StatisticalFunctions.cs ⊅ ×
StatsExcel                              StatsExcel.StatisticalFunctions                    DescriptiveStatistics(double[] data, object[] keys)
  55          // ...
  58      [ExcelFunction(Name = "StatisticalFunctions.DescriptiveStatistics",
  59                  Description = "Retrieve a package of descriptive statistics for the input data",
  60                  HelpTopic = "")]
  61      public static object[,] DescriptiveStatistics(
  62          [ExcelArgument(Description = "Array of data values")] double[] data,
  63          [ExcelArgument(Description = "Array of keys (optional)")] object[] keys
  64          )
  65      {
  66          object[,] obj = null;
  67          try
  68          {
  69              List<double> _data = new List<double>(data);
  70              List<string> _keys = ConvertKeys(keys);
  71
  72              Dictionary<string, double> results = Statistics.DescriptiveStatistics(_data, _keys);
  73              obj = ResultsToObject(results);
  74          }
  75          catch(Exception e)
  76          {
  77              obj = ReportException(e);
  78          }
  79          return obj;
  80      }
```

From Listing 4-6, we can see that the function is described by the `ExcelFunction[]` attribute. We can supply a `Name`, a `Description`, and a `HelpTopic` reference. From Excel's point of view, the function is called by the value in the `Name` attribute. So here it is called `"StatisticalFunctions.DescriptiveStatistics"`. We try to keep the namespace and the function name unique as we want to coexist with other functions present in Excel. In addition to the name, there are a number of attributes that we can use to describe our function. Specifically, we use the `ExcelArgument[]` attribute to describe the parameters. In this case, the function takes an array of doubles (`double[] data`) and an array of string keys which we pass as objects (`object[] keys`). The function returns an array (`object[,]`).

Type Conversion

In general, we need to convert the Excel types to types our wrapper functions understand. Since we decided on List<double> for the data, we take advantage of the fact that the .NET framework allows us to construct the List directly from an array, so there is less work to do in the conversion code. For the keys, we are passed an object array, which could contain strings and other data. Therefore, we need to properly convert the keys. Listing 4-7 shows how we do this.

Listing 4-7. Converting an object array of keys to a list of strings

```
StatisticalFunctions.cs  ⊕ ✕
 StatsExcel                    ▼  StatsExcel.StatisticalFunctions                  ▼    ConvertKeys(object[] keys)
27
28            public static List<string> ConvertKeys(object[] keys)
29            {
30                List<string> _keys = new List<string>();
31                if (keys != null)
32                {
33                    for (int i = 0; i < keys.Length; ++i)
34                    {
35                        var key = keys[i].ToString();
36                        if(key == "ExcelDna.Integration.ExcelEmpty" || key == "ExcelDna.Integration.ExcelMissing")
37                        { }
38                        else
39                        {
40                            _keys.Add(key);
41                        }
42                    }
43                }
44                return _keys;
45            }
```

The function first constructs an empty List<string>. Then we check if the input keys array is valid. If so, we iterate over the input keys converting them to strings. If the conversion fails, an exception will be thrown. We deal with exceptions in the following. If the key is non-empty, we add it to the list and return this to the caller when complete.

For the return value from DescriptiveStatistics, we need to convert the results Dictionary<string, double> into a two-column array of objects (object[,]). In our case, it will contain strings in the first column and doubles in the second. Listing 4-8 shows the conversion function.

Listing 4-8. Converting the package of results into a two-column array

```
StatisticalFunctions.cs  ⊣  ✕
StatsExcel                      ▾  StatsExcel.StatisticalFunctions                          ▾  ResultsToObject(Dictionary<string, double> results)
  16  ⊞      // ...
  19  ⊟      public static object[,] ResultsToObject(Dictionary<string, double> results)
  20         {
  21             object[,] o = new object[results.Keys.Count, 2 /* columns */];
  22  ⊟         for (int i = 0; i < results.Keys.Count; ++i)
  23             {
  24                 var element = results.ElementAt(i);
  25                 o[i, 0] = element.Key;
  26                 o[i, 1] = element.Value;
  27             }
  28             return o;
  29         }
```

The first line creates an object array using the dimensions of the keys collections of the results parameter. Then we iterate over the results items extracting each key-value pair and assigning them to the object array. This is then returned to the caller.

Build and Run

The project should build without warnings or errors. If you set the StatsExcel project as the Startup Project, then you will be able to run the code immediately. Excel will start, and our generated *xll* will be loaded. If you want to run the add-in outside of the Visual Studio solution, double-click the file *StatsExcel-AddIn64.xll* located in either the *\StatsExcel\bin\Debug* or the *\StatsExcel\bin\Release* directory. Note that because the StatsExcel project references the StatsCLR project, the *StatsCLR.dll* is copied into this directory. The first time you run the add-in, Excel will prompt you to confirm that you want to enable this add-in for this session. If you want to avoid this prompt on subsequent runs, you can set the path to the add-in as a trusted location using Excel's Trust Center available from the Options menu.

Once Excel has started, open the file *..\Data\StatsCLRTest.xlsx*. This file contains two worksheets: "Basic Functionality" tests both the `DescriptiveStatistics` and the `LinearRegression` functions. For the `DescriptiveStatistics`, we define two ranges, 'xs' and 'ys', and use these to compute the descriptive statistics. The results are compared against hard-coded values. If you change one of the input values, you should observe some test failures. We also test the `DescriptiveStatistics` function by passing in the individual labels and comparing the results with the equivalent Excel function. Finally, we test the `LinearRegression` function. This is shown in Figure 4-7.

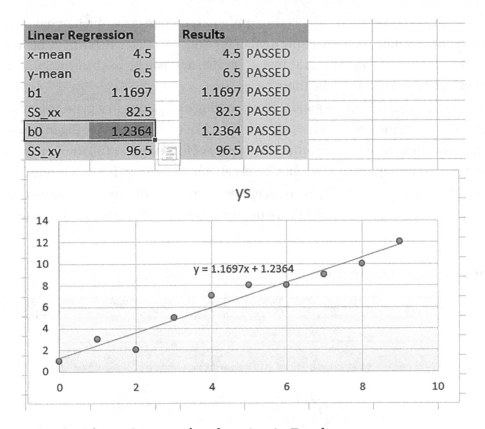

Figure 4-7. *The LinearRegression function in Excel*

Beneath the results, we plot the data and add a trendline. We can see that the regression equation displayed on the graph has the same intercept (b0) and slope (b1) coefficients that we have obtained.

The "Statistical Tests" worksheet exercises the TTest functionality. We check the summary data t-test, and both the one-sample and two-sample t-test. In the latter two cases, we display boxplots to indicate the differences in the means of the respective datasets. In both cases, it is clear that the respective means are significantly different, and this is confirmed by the pval of the t-tests (the probability that this difference would have been observed by chance).

Exception Handling

We should take care to ensure that exceptions are not propagated from our code into Excel as this might cause Excel to "crash," which is extremely undesirable. We know that the C++ layer will throw exceptions under certain conditions, specifically a std::invalid_argument if the data is not present or if there is insufficient data to perform an operation. We also know that, in the StatsCLR layer, these have been translated to System::InvalidOperationException, and will be re-thrown. So, in the StatsExcel layer, we should handle these exceptions.

In reality, Excel-DNA does a good job of handling exceptions in a generic way – it displays a #VALUE in the cell. In our case, we would like to display the string information. Under normal circumstances, we return the results of the function call into an object array. We take advantage of the fact that Excel can handle both string and numeric data in the returned object array. When an exception is thrown, we assign the result of the exception to the object array. For this we use the function ReportException, shown in Listing 4-9.

Listing 4-9. Reporting an exception

```
StatisticalFunctions.cs  ⊄  ✕
 StatsExcel                    ▼  StatsExcel.StatisticalFunctions                    ▼
    49
    50        static object[,] ReportException(Exception e)
    51        {
    52            object[,] obj = new object[1, 2];
    53            obj[0, 0] = "Exception: ";
    54            obj[0, 1] = e.Message;
    55            return obj;
    56        }
```

When an exception is thrown, we create a 1x2 array and populate the second column with the exception information. If we attempt to call the StatisticalTests.TTest function with no parameters, we see the following output:

"Error in function boost::math::students_t_distribution<double>::students_t_distribution: Degrees of freedom argument is -1, but must be > 0 !"

The result is not pretty, but it is informative. It is worth noting that if you call the function with empty parameter(s) you get back #VALUE!s. If you call the function with an empty array (cells with no data), this is passed along as an array of doubles initialized to 0, which, in the case of some functions, may be acceptable. If you pass in too few data points to the underlying C++ function GetDescriptiveStatistics, for example (it requires at least four to compute kurtosis, and three for skew), you get a message about "Insufficient data to perform the operation", which is the correct exception thrown from the C++ layer.

Debugging

Finally, a brief word about debugging. Debugging from inside Visual Studio is no more difficult than setting a breakpoint on the line we want to debug. This allows us to view the arguments being passed into the function, and to check that both the type and dimensions of the arguments correspond to the function signature. A mismatch here is a common source of runtime errors. In addition, we can set the flag "Enable native code debugging" to allow us to debug into the native C++ layer (from Excel), under Project settings ➤ Debug. With this, we can check that the values we are returning to Excel correspond to the declared return type in the function signature. Any issue can be investigated and resolved quickly.

Summary

In this chapter, we have demonstrated a number of use cases involving the StatsCLR component. We first looked at a basic C# console application. In addition to simply test-driving the statistical functions and classes, we incorporated functionality from Accord.NET. The examples may appear artificial and simplistic. However, the important point is that we were able to leverage the functionality from a different .NET component, alongside ours. We also saw how to use reflection to dynamically inspect the contents of an assembly. This also demonstrated that the StatsCLR component is a "proper" .NET assembly. What this means is that we can participate completely in the .NET type system. And this in turn facilitates other clients using our library. Finally, we connected the StatsCLR wrapper to Excel using Excel-DNA. Apart from allowing us to leverage Excel as a hosting environment, our component can seamlessly interoperate with other .NET components.

Additional Resources

The following links provide some additional background information for this chapter:

- For a more detailed discussion of assemblies in .NET, the following
  article is recommended: https://docs.microsoft.com/en-us/
  dotnet/standard/assembly/.

- The following document describes in detail how the .NET runtime locates assemblies: `https://docs.microsoft.com/en-us/dotnet/framework/configure-apps/specify-assembly-location`.

- There are a number of approaches to getting Excel to communicate with C++. Developing Excel XLLs is probably the most basic and is described in detail here: `https://docs.microsoft.com/en-us/office/client-developer/excel/developing-excel-xlls`. Other approaches include VSTO (`https://docs.microsoft.com/en-us/visualstudio/vsto/getting-started-programming-vsto-add-ins?view=vs-2019`) and Office add-ins.

- The Excel-DNA documentation can be found here: `https://docs.excel-dna.net/`. The "getting started" document is recommended (`https://docs.excel-dna.net/getting-started/`).

Exercises

The exercises that follow deal with the StatsExcel client and how it uses the new functionality that we have exposed via the StatsCLR component and also the functionality that we have made available transparently in the native C++ code.

1) Update the *StatsCLRTest.xlsx* sheets to display and check the new values for the `LinearRegression` coefficients.

- Add `SS_yy`, `r` and `r2` to the outputs (resizing the array as required).

- Update the test results so that they all pass.

2) In the StatsExcel project, add functions to perform a z-test. We follow the example of the t-test functions so that we end up with three new functions: `StatisticalFunctions.SummaryDataZTest`, `StatisticalFunctions.OneSampleZTest`, and `StatisticalFunctions.TwoSampleZtest`.

The steps required are as follows:

- Clone the existing functions and adapt them.

- Add a new worksheet to *StatsCLRTest.xlsx* (or make a copy of the existing Statistical Tests worksheet). Test the functions using datasets with expected values.

3) Add a function to *StatisticalFunctions.cs* called `StatisticalFunctions.`
`MovingAverage`. This will take three parameters: an array of dates, an array of
observations, and a window size parameter. As previously, this function is somewhat
more involved because we need to handle the conversion from `doubles` (supplied by
Excel) to a list of `DateTime` objects which our function expects. We also need to return
the resulting moving average series as a single column array of `doubles`.

Before adding the `MovingAverage` function, add the conversion code. The first
function converts the array of `doubles` (representing dates) into a `List<DateTime>`. This
can be implemented as follows:

```
public static List<DateTime> ToDateTime(double[] dates)
{
        List<DateTime> output = new List<DateTime>();
        for (int i = 0; i < dates.Length; ++i)
        {
                output.Add(DateTime.FromOADate(dates[i]));
        }
        return output;
}
```

The second function converts the `List<double>` results package to a one-column
object array. This can be implemented as follows:

```
public static object[,] ResultsToObject(List<double> results)
{
        object[,] o = new object[results.Count, 1 /* column */];
        for (int i = 0; i < results.Count; ++i)
        {
                var val = results.ElementAt(i);
                if (Double.IsNaN(val))
                        o[i, 0] = ExcelDna.Integration.ExcelError.ExcelErrorNA;
                else
                        o[i, 0] = val;
        }
        return o;
}
```

With this in place, add the MovingAverage function. The prototype is as follows:

```
[ExcelFunction(Name = "StatisticalFunctions.MovingAverage",
Description = "Compute a moving average from a set of data.",
HelpTopic = "")]
public static object[,] MovingAverage(
[ExcelArgument(Description = "Array of dates")] double[] dates,
[ExcelArgument(Description = "Array of observations")] double[] observations,
[ExcelArgument(Description = "Window")] int window
)
{
    // ...
}
```

- Convert the input parameters into types that the TimeSeries class understands. Create an instance of the C++/CLI TimeSeries class passing it the parameters. Request a MovingAverage and return the results into the object array. Remember to handle exceptions.

- Rebuild the StatsExcel project and test the new MovingAverage function. Add a new worksheet called Time Series. Use the same data as we used for the unit tests. Test the function in Excel. Excel has its own moving average calculation (under Data Analysis).[2] Compare the values produced by Excel to this implementation. They should be identical.

---

[2] This requires installation of the Analysis ToolPak.

PART III

R and Rcpp

CHAPTER 5

Building an R Package

Introduction

In this chapter and the next, we connect our simple C++ library of statistical functions to R. We do this by creating an R package using Rcpp. We then use this wrapper component to expose the functionality we want. This chapter focuses on both the project setup and the mechanics of building packages with RStudio. The following chapter focuses on the details of using Rcpp as a framework for connecting C++ and R.

The project setup in this case is slightly more involved than previously. In general terms, we require the standard environment for building a CRAN[1] package. More specifically, the development environment needs to use a suitable compiler. Because the outputs produced by different C++ compilers (GCC, MSVC, and so on) are not all the same, it is not possible to mix the generated object code from different compilers. The result, from our narrow practitioner perspective, is that we need to build a version of the C++ library of statistical functions with a different compiler/linker. Specifically, the GNU Compiler Collection (GCC) has to be used along with the corresponding g++ compiler (gcc) for the C++ language. This is in order to build an ABI (Application Binary Interface)-compatible component that will be hosted in R and which interoperates in the R environment.

A brief outline of the steps involved is as follows:

1. Install the required gcc tools.

2. Setup and build a new static library (using CodeBlocks) from the same sources as before. The library output is *libStatsLib.a*.

---

[1] CRAN (Comprehensive R Archive Network) is an official repository of R packages and documentation for R (`https://cran.r-project.org/`).

© Adam Gladstone 2022
A. Gladstone, *C++ Software Interoperability for Windows Programmers*,
https://doi.org/10.1007/978-1-4842-7966-3_5

91

3. Create the Rcpp project in RStudio (*StatsR*).

4. Configure the Rcpp project to use the new static library.

This will give us a working wrapper shell. Later on, we look at how the functionality is added. Unlike in previous chapters, we focus more on the toolchain (CodeBlocks, Rtools, and RStudio) in this chapter. We leave writing the Rcpp layer, and building and testing the functionality until the next chapter.

Prerequisites

Rtools

Rtools is a suite of tools for building R packages on Windows and includes the gcc compiler. The installer for Rtools is available from `https://cran.r-project.org/bin/windows/Rtools/`. You should install the 64-bit version of Rtools: *rtools40-x86_64.exe*. It is important to note that to install Rtools 4.0 you will need version 4.0.0 of R or above. After completing the installation, ensure that the `RTOOLS40_HOME` environment variable is set to the *rtools* directory. Also, add the *rtools* directory to the `PATH` environment variable. It is also possible to install Rtools directly from inside RStudio, using the command: `install.Rtools()`. This installs the latest version of Rtools. The following link gives instructions on how to do this: `https://rdrr.io/cran/installr/man/install.Rtools.html`. To check that Rtools has been installed correctly, open a PowerShell prompt and type `gcc --version` to display the program version information.

Installing CodeBlocks

In reality, installing CodeBlocks is not a prerequisite, it is a convenience. The installer is available from `www.codeblocks.org/downloads/binaries`. Our goal is to build an ABI-compliant static library with the gcc toolchain, and there are several ways to achieve this. If you are comfortable building libraries manually using makefiles or you prefer to use CMake to configure a build environment using the gcc toolchain, you do not need to use CodeBlocks. Appendix B contains basic instructions on configuring a Visual Studio

CMake project *StatsLibCM* to build the library output we require. On the other hand, if you prefer Visual Studio Code as your C++ development environment, this can also be configured to work with GCC using MinGW. For further information, see the Additional resources section at the end of the chapter.

Because CodeBlocks is already configured for cross-platform C++ development using gcc, we will continue to use it here. In addition, CodeBlocks provides a wide variety of useful project types and several build targets (static-link library, dynamic-link library, for example). Moreover, the debugging support (including setting breakpoints and watch variables) is easier than using gdb from a console session.

CodeBlocks
Toolchain Setup

Open up CodeBlocks. Go to Settings ➤ Compiler ... . Under the Selected compiler, select GNU GCC Compiler and configure the version g++ targeting C++17. Figure 5-1 shows the Global compiler settings.

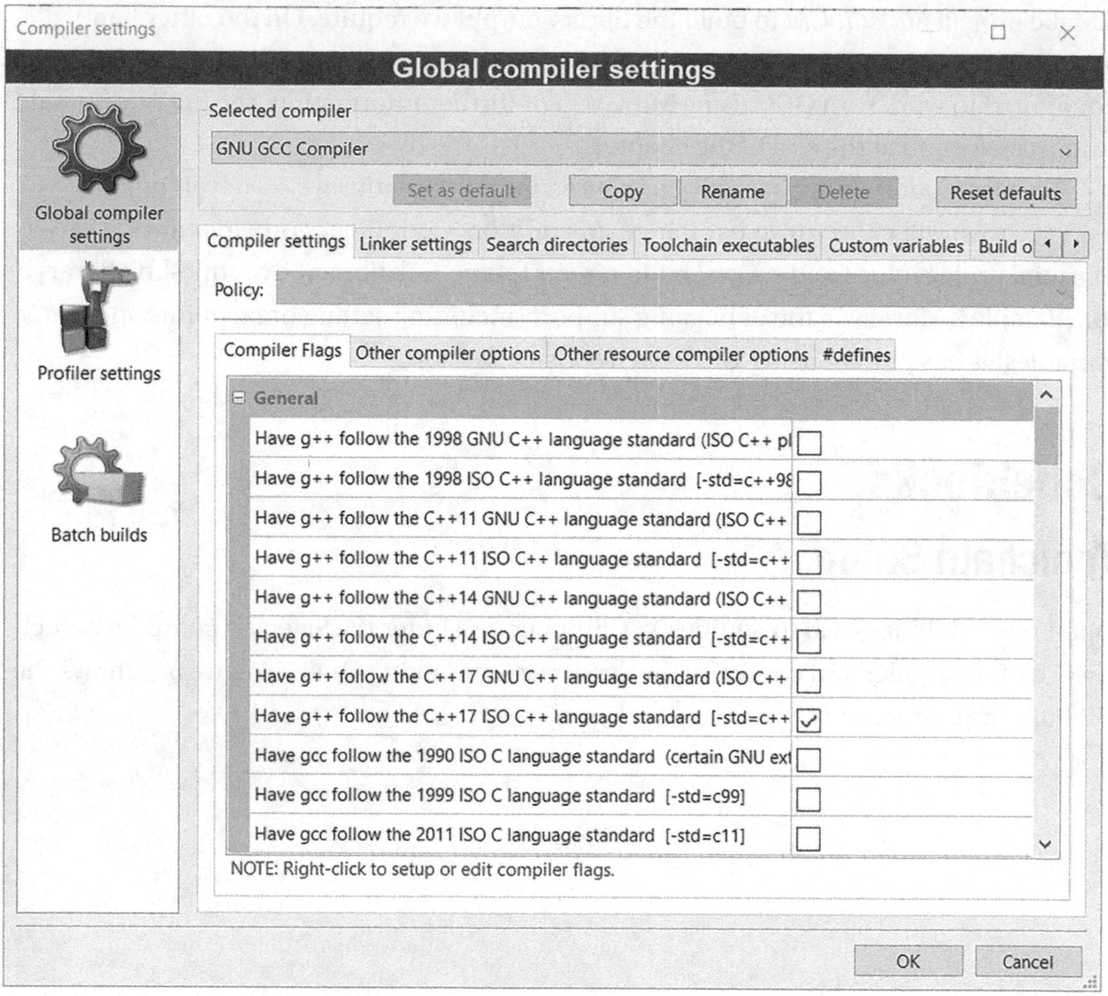

Figure 5-1. *Compiler settings in CodeBlocks*

In addition to the General settings (shown in Figure 5-1), there are a number of useful options for controlling aspects of the compilation. Specifically, there are options for debugging, profiling, warnings, optimization, and CPU architecture. For this project we do not make use of any of these options, but it is useful to know they exist.

Next, in the Toolchain executables tab, click the Auto Detect button. This should fill in the path to the compiler's installation directory, for example, *D:\Program Files\ mingw-w64\x86_64-8.1.0-posix-seh-rt_v6-rev0\mingw64*. If this isn't the case, click the *".."* button, and manually select the MinGW directory (under which the gcc tools are located). Note that CodeBlocks itself installs the MinGW toolset. So, in addition to Rtools, you may have a second installation of MinGW. I have two versions of the MinGW packages – one with gcc 8.1.0 from CodeBlocks and one with gcc 8.3.0 from Rtools. This does not cause a problem since the outputs from both are ABI compatible. The MinGW installation from CodeBlocks puts the directory into the PATH environment variable, so this is what we use to build with. You can, however, change this to use the path to Rtools if you prefer.

Fill in the rest of the tools as shown in Figure 5-2.

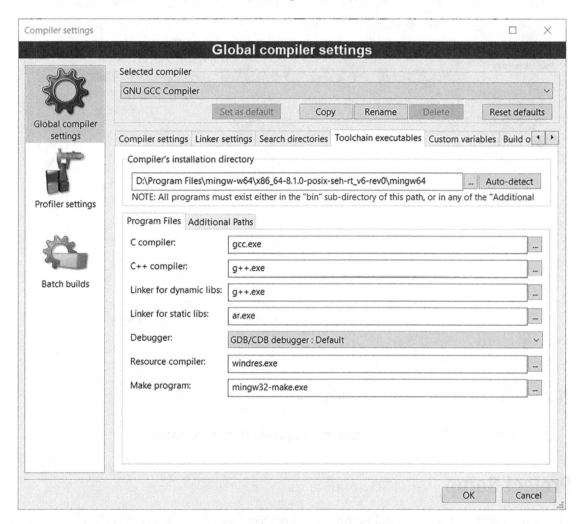

Figure 5-2. *Toolchain executables*

Finally, under the Search Directories tab, add the path to the *boost_1_76_0* directory. Figure 5-3 shows the setting we use.

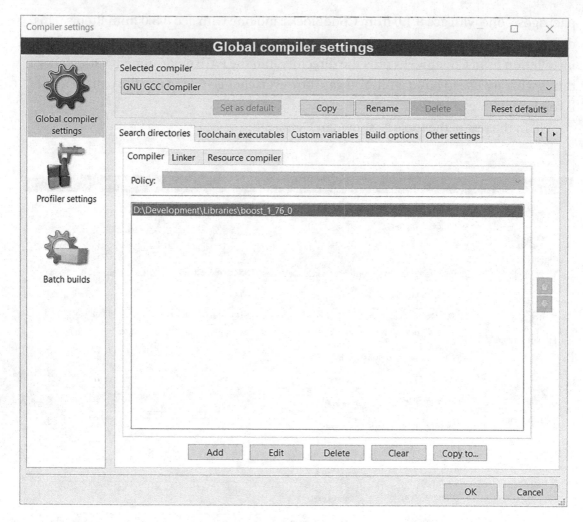

Figure 5-3. *Setting the search path to use Boost*

When you have finished configuring this, press OK to save any changes.

Project Setup

The StatsLibCB directory contains the CodeBlocks project file (*StatsLibCB.cbp*). The project uses the Static Library template. The static library is based on the same C++ sources as previously, located in the *\Common* directory. Open the project in CodeBlocks. Right-click on the project node and select Project properties as shown in Figure 5-4.

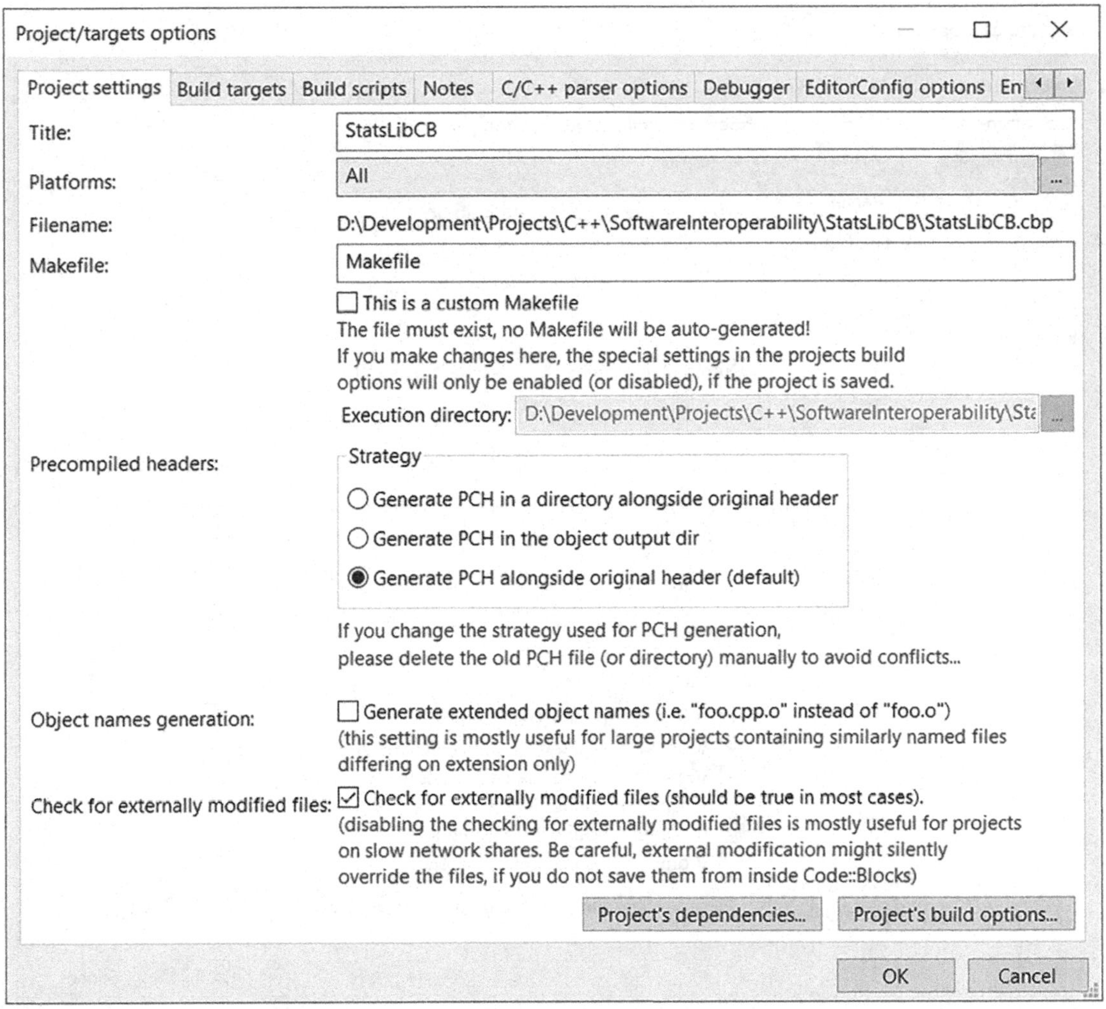

Figure 5-4. *Project settings*

The overall project settings are straightforward. This page (Figure 5-4) gives options relating to the object file generation, *pch* file, platforms, and execution directory. We have not made any changes here. Select the Build targets page and check that the (Debug and Release) build targets are shown as in Figure 5-5.

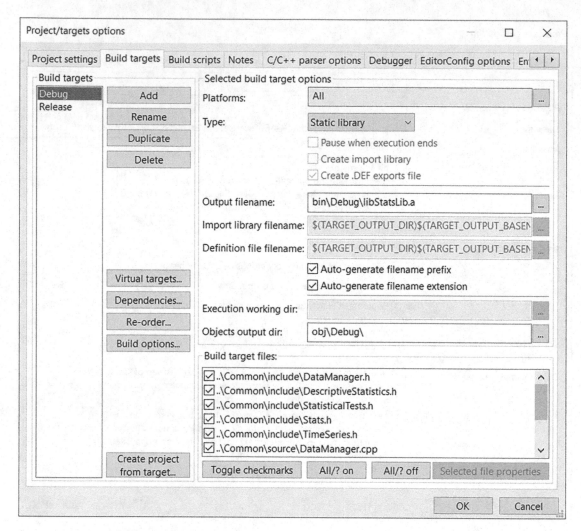

Figure 5-5. *Build targets for libStatsLib*

Looking at Figure 5-5, we can see that the type of the project is set to Static library. The Output filename is *libStatsLib.a* (both *Debug* and *Release*). At the bottom of Figure 5-5, we can see the Build target files that we have added. Click OK to save the settings. The project environment should look like Figure 5-6.

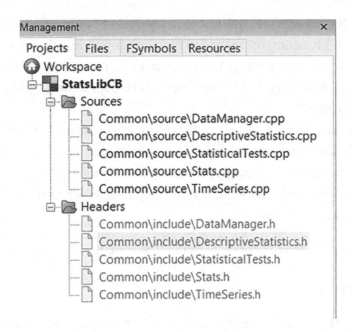

Figure 5-6. *The project node with the source and include files*

Depending on how the StatsLibCB workspace node is being displayed (right-click on the node for various options), your view of the project files may be slightly different. At this stage, the project is ready to build. From the Build menu, select Build (Ctrl+F9). Build both the debug and release versions of the library. The Build log tool window displays the command line passed to the compiler and linker. The project should build without warnings or errors, and the library (*libStatsLib.a*) should be located in the output directory corresponding to the selected build target.

R/RStudio Packages

Background

For this section, you will need to have RStudio up and running. RStudio is the IDE of choice for hosting the R environment and developing applications using the R language. We could have used the more basic RGui; however, RStudio provides better facilities, specifically when it comes to building R packages. So, having built the ABI-compliant statistics library successfully, we are now ready to create an R package that uses it.

On Windows, R packages are dynamic-link libraries. They can be loaded dynamically using the `dyn.load()` function using the full filename (including the *dll* extension) or, more typically, using the `library()` command for installed (registered) packages. Among other things, RStudio provides a convenient IDE for managing the installation and loading of packages.

To communicate with packages, the R language and environment provides a low-level C-style API (application programming interface). Once a package has been loaded, users can call functions in the package, pass parameters, and get results back. What this means is that once we have built the *StatsR.dll* as a package, we could load it and execute the following command, for example:

```
> .Call("_StatsR_get_descriptive_statistics", c(0,1,2,3,4,5,6,7,8,9),
c("StdErr"))
   StdErr 0.9574271
```

This calls the `get_descriptive_statistics` function with two parameters passed as collections: the data and a single key, "StdErr". The results are returned as expected. The actual function name we use in making the call `_StatsR_get_descriptive_statistics` is the C-style exported function name. We could get this from inspecting the *StatsR.dll* using a tool like *Depends.exe*.

However, this API is quite low-level and not ideal for extended development. Our intention here is to expose a (limited) number of functions from the underlying C++ statistics library. Using the C-style API approach, we would need to declare all the functions to be of type `extern "C"` SEXP. This is a pointer to a SEXPREC or Simple EXPression RECord, an opaque pointer type used by R. Furthermore, the parameters would have to be typed as pointers to S EXPression objects (SEXP). Using the C-style API does allow us to exchange data and objects between C++ and R, but it is not a practical proposition for more complex C++ development.

The Rcpp framework solves this issue. The Rcpp layer sits above the `.Call()` API and shields the C++ developer from needing to use the low-level SEXP types. Rcpp provides an interface that automatically translates standard C++ into calls to the low-level API. From the point of view of development, Rcpp allows us to use standard C++ for the wrapper component.

Building a Package with Rcpp

Installing Rcpp

The Rcpp package can be installed by running the R command: `install.packages("Rcpp")`. Alternatively, from the RStudio menu, we can use the Tools ➤ Install Packages... command. Once completed, we are ready to build an Rcpp package. From inside RStudio, open the StatsR project: File ➤ Open Project .... The *StatsR.Rproj* file is located in the *StatsR* directory under the *SoftwareInteroperability* directory.

The Project Files

The RStudio IDE provides the facility to create an Rcpp project directly. StatsR was created using File ➤ New Project, and in the New Project Wizard, selecting New Directory, then "R Package using Rcpp" and a directory name. With this, the boilerplate files are generated. We could have generated the required package files from scratch or we could have used the command `Rcpp.package.skeleton` to generate the project files. In our case, the Rcpp project template generates the files in several subdirectories under the *StatsR* project directory. The files are listed as follows with a brief description of each:

- *StatsR.proj*

  This is the RStudio project file.

- *DESCRIPTION*

  This file contains descriptive information about this package (Package name, Type, Version, Date, Author, and so on). It also contains metadata about the package dependencies. See the Additional Resources section for links to more detailed information about package metadata.

- *NAMESPACE*

  This file contains three directives. Firstly, `useDynLib(...)` ensures that the dynamic library that is part of this package is loaded and registered. Next, the `importFrom(...)` directive imports variables from other packages (other than baseR, which are always imported). In this case, we import variables from the Rcpp and the evalCpp packages. The final directive, `exportPattern(...)`, declares which

101

identifiers should be globally visible from the namespace of this
package. The default is to export all identifiers that start with a letter.
This is defined in the regular expression.

- *\man\StatsR-package.Rd*

  This is an R markdown template file that is used for describing the
  package. You can edit this in RStudio. Pressing the Preview button
  displays the formatted contents in the Help window.

- *\R\RcppExports.R*

  This file contains the R language function calls generated by Rcpp.

- *\src\RcppExports.cpp*

  This file contains the C++ functions generated by Rcpp.

- *\src\Makevars.win*

  This file contains the configuration options for the compiler/linker.

- *\src\StatsR.cpp*

  This is the main file we will be working with in this chapter and
  contains boilerplate code.

Editing the Makefile

In terms of packaging, up to now we have been working inwards from both sides, as it
were. On one side, we have rebuilt our statistical functions library as *libStatsLib.a*. On
the other side, we have created a *StatsR* project using Rcpp. Now, we need to link the
C++ statistical functions library into the Rcpp project. To do this, we need to update
Makevars.win. This file can be found in the *\src* directory. *Makevars.win* is the Windows
makefile for this project. It overrides the default build configuration file *Makeconf*. For
reference, this file can be found by running the command `file.path(R.home("etc"),`
`"Makeconf")`. It contains all the settings for compiling and linking using the gcc
toolchain, so should be treated with some caution. For this project, the configuration is
much simpler. We only use a single flag:

- `PKG_LIBS`: This flag is used to link in additional libraries (such as
  libStatsLib.a).

Two other flags of interest, depending on the build target, are

- PKG_CXXFLAGS: This flag can be used to set additional debug or release options. For debugging, we build with debug information for gdb (-ggdb), the zero-optimization level (-o0), and the warning level (-Wall). For release builds, we remove these settings.

- PKG_CPPFLAGS: These relate to preprocessor flags and can be used to set additional include directories with -I.

The Additional Resources section provides links to more detailed descriptions of the flags and their usage. Returning to *Makevars.win*, we have added the following lines at the bottom of the makefile:

```
## Directory where the static library is output
PKG_LIBS=<your path>/SoftwareInteroperability/StatsLibCB/bin/Release/
libStatsLib.a
```

This will tell the linker to link with the release version of the *libStatsLib* library. Save your changes.

Boilerplate Code

Still in the *\src* directory, open the file *StatsR.cpp*. There is some useful generated boilerplate code here that we will use to check the build process. Listing 5-1 shows the code.

Listing 5-1. Boilerplate C++ function in the StatsR package

```
StatsR.cpp ×
         Source on Save
 1   #include <Rcpp.h>
 2
 3   using namespace Rcpp;
 4
 5   //' Display the library name and version number.
 6   //'
 7   //' @param
 8   //' @export
 9   // [[Rcpp::export]]
10   String library_version() {
11
12       return String("StatsR, version 1.0");
13   }
14
15
```

In this file, we define a single C++ function called `library_version` that returns a hard-coded string. There are a couple of features that are worth highlighting in this small example.

Firstly, at the top of the file, we include *Rcpp.h*. This is the main Rcpp header. You can find this under *\library\Rcpp* in your R distribution (e.g., *D:\R\R-4.0.3\library*) alongside the rest of the source code. Rcpp is quite an extensive package (some 300+ files) and has a lot of facilities that are well worth exploring. The documentation directory (*Rcpp\doc*) contains a number of useful bitesize reference documents that are worth referring to. We barely scratch the surface in the two chapters on R in this book.

Secondly, of note is the attribute

```
// [[Rcpp::export]].
```

This indicates that we want to make this C++ function available to R. The function itself is quite simple. It constructs a `String` object and returns it to the caller.

The RStudio IDE is good for writing and developing R scripts. However, for C++ development it is less useful, especially when it comes to being able to read through source code or go to definitions of types (like `String` in the preceding example). While not absolutely critical, it is nice to be able to right-click on a symbol and jump to the definition (if possible). This also makes both navigating around the source code and investigating any compilation errors related to type conversions slightly easier.

With this in mind, a quick and non-intrusive workaround to achieve this using Visual Studio Code is the following. Open the *StatsR* directory in Visual Studio Code (File ➤ Open Folder …), then open the *StatsR.cpp* file. For this to work, you will need to have installed the VSCode C++ plugin ("C/C++ for Visual Studio Code"). Edit the plugin configuration file (*<your path>\SoftwareInteroperability\StatsR\.vscode\c_cpp_properties.json*) to look for the sources in the Rcpp location and the root include directory. Add the "`configurations`" section in Listing 5-2 to the *c_cpp_properties.json* properties file.

Listing 5-2. Adding include paths to the c_cpp_properties.json file in VSCode

```
"configurations": [
    {
        "name": "Win32",
        "includePath": [
            "${workspaceFolder}/**",
            "D:/R/R-4.0.3/library/Rcpp/include/**",
            "D:/R/R-4.0.3/include/**"
        ],
```

With this in place, you can right-click on symbols (or press F12) and jump to the definition as shown in Figure 5-7.

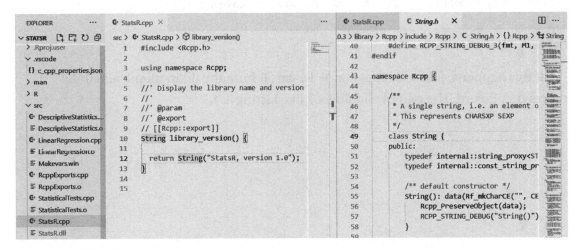

Figure 5-7. *Using Visual Studio Code to navigate the Rcpp source files*

Looking at Figure 5-7, it turns out that the String class encapsulates a CHARSXP – an S-expression pointer of type char (roughly speaking).

Building StatsR

Returning to the function library_version: we will use this simple function to test the build end to end. We should be able to call this function from the minimal R script in Listing 5-3.

Listing 5-3. A simple test R script

```
library(StatsR)                # Load the library
res = StatsR::library_version() # Retrieve the library version
res                            # Display it
```

Click Build ➤ Clean and Rebuild (or from the Build menu in the Build pane). It sometimes happens that the current R session is active, for example, if you have reloaded the environment when opening a project. This will result in the Clean and Rebuild displaying a message that the library is in use, similar to the following:

```
ERROR: cannot remove earlier installation, is it in use?
* removing 'D:/R/R-4.0.3/library/StatsR'
* restoring previous 'D:/R/R-4.0.3/library/StatsR'
...
Exited with status 1.
```

If this happens, just select Session ➤ Restart R from the main menu, and then proceed as before. The output should look like Listing 5-4.

Listing 5-4. Clean and Rebuild output

```
Environment   History   Connections   Build   Git   Tutorial                              ─ □
⤒ Install and Restart   ☑ Check   ⚙ More ▾                                                    ⟋
==> Rcpp::compileAttributes()

* Updated R/RcppExports.R

==> Rcmd.exe INSTALL --preclean --no-multiarch --with-keep.source StatsR

* installing to library 'D:/R/R-4.0.3/library'
* installing *source* package 'StatsR' ...
** using staged installation
** libs
/mingw64/bin/g++    -std=gnu++17 -I"D:/R/R-4.0.3/include" -DNDEBUG  -I'D:/R/R-4.0.3/library/Rcpp/include'
 -ggdb -O0 -Wall    -O2 -Wall  -mfpmath=sse -msse2 -mstackrealign -c DescriptiveStatistics.cpp -o Descriptiv
eStatistics.o
/mingw64/bin/g++    -std=gnu++17 -I"D:/R/R-4.0.3/include" -DNDEBUG  -I'D:/R/R-4.0.3/library/Rcpp/include'
 -ggdb -O0 -Wall    -O2 -Wall  -mfpmath=sse -msse2 -mstackrealign -c LinearRegression.cpp -o LinearRegressio
n.o
/mingw64/bin/g++    -std=gnu++17 -I"D:/R/R-4.0.3/include" -DNDEBUG  -I'D:/R/R-4.0.3/library/Rcpp/include'
 -ggdb -O0 -Wall    -O2 -Wall  -mfpmath=sse -msse2 -mstackrealign -c RcppExports.cpp -o RcppExports.o
/mingw64/bin/g++    -std=gnu++17 -I"D:/R/R-4.0.3/include" -DNDEBUG  -I'D:/R/R-4.0.3/library/Rcpp/include'
 -ggdb -O0 -Wall    -O2 -Wall  -mfpmath=sse -msse2 -mstackrealign -c StatisticalTests.cpp -o StatisticalTest
s.o
/mingw64/bin/g++    -std=gnu++17 -I"D:/R/R-4.0.3/include" -DNDEBUG  -I'D:/R/R-4.0.3/library/Rcpp/include'
 -ggdb -O0 -Wall    -O2 -Wall  -mfpmath=sse -msse2 -mstackrealign -c StatsR.cpp -o StatsR.o
/mingw64/bin/g++ -shared -s -static-libgcc -o StatsR.dll tmp.def DescriptiveStatistics.o LinearRegression.o
 RcppExports.o StatisticalTests.o StatsR.o D:/Development/Projects/C++/SoftwareInteroperability/StatsLibCB/
bin/Debug/libStatsLib.a -LD:/R/R-4.0.3/bin/x64 -lR
installing to D:/R/R-4.0.3/library/00LOCK-StatsR/00new/StatsR/libs/x64
** R
** byte-compile and prepare package for lazy loading
** help
*** installing help indices
  converting help for package 'StatsR'
    finding HTML links ...    StatsR-package                               html    done

** building package indices
** testing if installed package can be loaded from temporary location
** testing if installed package can be loaded from final location
** testing if installed package keeps a record of temporary installation path
* DONE (StatsR)
Making 'packages.html' ... done
```

Listing 5-4 shows in detail the steps taken in the build process. As might be expected, the "Clean and Rebuild" process is somewhat involved. The first stage is the call to `Rcpp::compileAttributes()`. This inspects the C++ functions in the \src directory and looks for attributes of the form `// [[Rcpp::export]]`. When it finds one, it generates both the C++ and the R code that is required to expose the function to R. These function wrappers are generated in *src/RcppExports.cpp* and *R/RcppExports.R* (note the different file extensions and locations). More specifically, Rcpp uses the export attribute to generate a function wrapper which maps an R function `library_version` to a C-style function call. This is the R call (found in *RcppExports.R*). Listing 5-5 shows the R function.

Listing 5-5. The R function stub generated from the `library_version` C++ code

```
RcppExports.R* ×
       Source on Save    Q    ✗ ▾
 ⚠ This document is read only.
 50
 51   #' Display the library name and version number.
 52   #'
 53   #' @param
 54   #' @export
 55 ▾ library_version <- function() {
 56       .Call(`_StatsR_library_version`)
 57 ▴ }
```

You can see that this uses the low-level `.Call()` interface that we described earlier. The corresponding C++ function is also generated in *RcppExports.cpp*. This is shown in Listing 5-6.

Listing 5-6. Low-level C++ code generated by Rcpp

```
// library_version
String library_version();
RcppExport SEXP _StatsR_library_version() {
BEGIN_RCPP
    Rcpp::RObject rcpp_result_gen;
    Rcpp::RNGScope rcpp_rngScope_gen;
    rcpp_result_gen = Rcpp::wrap(library_version());
    return rcpp_result_gen;
END_RCPP
}
```

The first line (after the comment) is the function signature of the C++ function. This is followed by the C-style API declaration. Inside the function, Rcpp has generated code to call the function and return the results. We will have more to say about the Rcpp code generated here in the following chapter.

In addition to the generated C++ function wrappers, *RcppExports.cpp* also contains the module definition. This is a mapping from the function name to an exported function address. It also contains information about the number of parameters. You should never need to use these files directly. Both files (*src/RcppExports.cpp* and *R/RcppExports.R*) are flagged as read-only. Modifying these files by hand is not recommended.

To summarize what is happening so far: we have written a C++ function `library_version` (in fact this was boilerplate code, but the process is the same); Rcpp has generated an R function and the low-level wrapper code that translates Rcpp types to low-level types understood by the R `.Call()` API.

After the file generation, the build process then builds a DLL and makes it available to R. It does this by installing the package in the package location. You can confirm this by looking in your R distribution under *library*. In our case, it is under *D:\R\R-4.0.3\library\StatsR*. Finally, the build process generates some documentation. You can configure the build process to use roxygen2, if you require. In this case, we stick with the default R markdown documentation. This is used to generate an html version of the documentation in the package location (*D:/R/R-4.0.3/library/StatsR/html/StatsR-package.html*).

If everything has gone to plan, we should now find a *StatsR.dll* in the project directory under *src*. And it should be loaded into the RStudio environment. You can confirm this by executing the command in Listing 5-7.

Listing 5-7. Obtaining a list of the loaded DLLs

```
> getLoadedDLLs()
                                                      Filename Dynamic.Lookup
base                                                      base           FALSE
methods          D:/R/R-4.0.3/library/methods/libs/x64/methods.dll     FALSE
utils                D:/R/R-4.0.3/library/utils/libs/x64/utils.dll     FALSE
grDevices    D:/R/R-4.0.3/library/grDevices/libs/x64/grDevices.dll     FALSE
graphics      D:/R/R-4.0.3/library/graphics/libs/x64/graphics.dll     FALSE
stats            D:/R/R-4.0.3/library/stats/libs/x64/stats.dll         FALSE
fansi            D:/R/R-4.0.3/library/fansi/libs/x64/fansi.dll         FALSE
glue                  D:/R/R-4.0.3/library/glue/libs/x64/glue.dll      FALSE
tools            D:/R/R-4.0.3/library/tools/libs/x64/tools.dll         FALSE
internet                D:/R/R-4.0.3/modules/x64/internet.dll          TRUE
(embedding)                                        (embedding)        FALSE
rlang            D:/R/R-4.0.3/library/rlang/libs/x64/rlang.dll         FALSE
testthat    D:/R/R-4.0.3/library/testthat/libs/x64/testthat.dll       FALSE
Rcpp                  D:/R/R-4.0.3/library/Rcpp/libs/x64/Rcpp.dll       TRUE
StatsR          D:/R/R-4.0.3/library/StatsR/libs/x64/StatsR.dll       FALSE
> |
```

The StatsR package appears at the bottom of the list of loaded dlls in Listing 5-7. Your output will look different depending on what is currently loaded. We can check that the version function works as expected by executing the following command:

```
> library_version()
```

The output should be: `[1] "StatsR, version 1.0"`.

In addition, we can inspect the functions that are available in the package, as follows:

```
> library(pkgload)
> StatsFunctions = names(pkg_env("StatsR"))
> as.data.frame(StatsFunctions)
                StatsFunctions
1          t_test_two_sample
2 get_descriptive_statistics
3          t_test_one_sample
4         t_test_summary_data
5              library_version
6            linear_regression
```

With this completed, we have a fully working Rcpp package which provides a wrapper around our C++ library of statistical functions.

Summary

We've covered quite a lot of ground in this chapter. We have (re)built the library of statistics functions using the gcc compiler/linker. We have also built the wrapper component, *StatsR.dll*. This is convenient, as it allows us to reuse the sources without change, while at the same time separating the wrapper component (*StatsR.dll*) from the underlying C++ code.

This chapter has focused on setting up the infrastructure required to build R packages that consume C++ functionality. It should be emphasized that this arrangement is only one of a number of possible ways of organizing the R package development and build process. With CodeBlocks open as our C++ development IDE, we can now develop C++ code, which we can compile and build into a static library (*libStatsLib.a*), for example. Then, in RStudio, we can use our Rcpp project (*StatsR*) to expose the C++ functions. We can build this into an R package and make the functionality available immediately in an R session. We now have the infrastructure for end-to-end C++ and R development. With this infrastructure in place, we are now in a position to look at using Rcpp. In the next chapter, we look in more detail at the Rcpp framework we use in the wrapper component and how the statistical functions are exposed to R via Rcpp.

Additional Resources

The following links provide some more information on the topics covered in this chapter:

- Detailed information on using GCC with MinGW under Visual Studio Code is available from `https://code.visualstudio.com/docs/cpp/config-mingw`. In addition to configuring Visual Studio Code to use the GCC C++ compiler (g++) and the GDB debugger from mingw-w64, the tutorial demonstrates compiling and debugging.

- The full documentation for CodeBlocks is available at `www.codeblocks.org/user-manual/`.

- For full details about package metadata, the following link is very useful: `https://r-pkgs.org/description.html`, particularly Chapter 8.

- If you are not familiar with GCC compiler settings and options, the following link provides a useful list: `https://caiorss.github.io/C-Cpp-Notes/compiler-flags-options.html`.

- For detailed information about the compiler/linker switches, see the section on Using Makevars: `https://cran.r-project.org/doc/manuals/r-devel/R-exts.html#Using-Makevars`. This document also gives a lot of useful information about writing R extensions. The following Stackoverflow post provides a useful summary: `https://stackoverflow.com/questions/43597632/understanding-the-contents-of-the-makevars-file-in-r-macros-variables-r-ma/43599233#43599233`.

Exercises

The exercises that follow mainly deal with the effects of adding code to the C++ codebase and building these changes in a library that we can use to then build an R package. The exercises are concerned with setting up the infrastructure for usage in R/RStudio.

1) Rebuild *libStatsLib.a* in preparation for use inside R/RStudio. The intention here is to recompile the code in the static library and make sure that we can link this to the StatsR project.

The steps to follow are

- Open the StatsLibCB project in CodeBlocks. The `TimeSeries` class is already incorporated as part of the project, so there is no need to do anything. Expand the Sources node and confirm that *TimeSeries.cpp* is present. Do the same for the header file. If you have added a `ZTest` class to the *StatisticalTests.h/StatisticalTests.cpp*, then they can be built immediately.

  On the other hand, if you have added the `ZTest` class in separate files, then you will need to add the files to the StatsLibCB project. To do this, select Project ➤ Properties, Build targets tab, and add them.

- Build both debug/release versions. They should build without warnings or errors. Check that the files are being compiled/linked.

- Open RStudio. Select Build ➤ Clean and Rebuild and check that the build (still) works without warnings or errors. Confirm that the StatsR package loads and works.

## CHAPTER 6

Exposing Functions Using Rcpp

Introduction

In the previous chapter, we built an R package using Rcpp. Moreover, using CodeBlocks, we established the infrastructure for developing and building our ABI-compliant library of statistical functions (*libStatsLib.a*), which we linked into our R package (*StatsR.dll*). For the moment, we have only used a single function, `library_version` (defined in *StatsR.cpp*). We used this to illustrate the build process and to test the communication between R and C++.

In this chapter, we look in detail at how to expose the functionality of the underlying statistical library. We first look at the descriptive statistics and linear regression functions. Then we examine RcppModules in the context of the statistical test classes. The final part of this chapter looks at using the component with other R packages. We cover testing, measuring performance, and debugging. The chapter ends with a small Shiny app demonstration.

The Conversion Layer

In the C++/CLI wrapper (Chapter 3), we spent some time developing an explicit conversion layer, where we put the functions to translate between the managed world and native C++ types. The approach taken by Rcpp means that we no longer need to do this. We make use of types defined in the Rcpp C++ namespace in addition to standard C++ types, and we let Rcpp generate the underlying code that allows communication

113

© Adam Gladstone 2022
A. Gladstone, *C++ Software Interoperability for Windows Programmers*,
https://doi.org/10.1007/978-1-4842-7966-3_6

between R and C++. This interface ensures that our underlying statistical library is kept separate and independent of Rcpp.

As pointed out in the previous chapter, the Rcpp namespace is quite extensive. It contains numerous functions and objects that shield us from the basic underlying C interface provided by R. We only use a small part of the functionality, concentrating particularly on `Rcpp::NumericVector`, `Rcpp::CharacterVector`, `Rcpp::List,` and `Rcpp::DataFrame`.

Code Organization

The C++ code in the StatsR project is organized under the project's *src* directory. This is where we locate the project's C++ compilable units. Under this directory, we have already seen the following:

- *StatsR.cpp*: Contains a boilerplate Rcpp C++ function

- *RcppExports.cpp*: Contains the generated C++ functions

- *Makevars.win*: Contains the Windows build configuration settings

In addition to the preceding list, we have the following three files, one for each of the functional areas we want to expose:

- *DescriptiveStatistics.cpp*

- *LinearRegression.cpp*

- *StatisticalTests.cpp*

This is a convenient way to organize the functionality, and we will deal with each of these in turn.

Descriptive Statistics
The Code

Listing 6-1 shows the code for the C++ wrapper function `get_descriptive_statistics`.

Listing 6-1. C++ code for the `DescriptiveStatistics` wrapper function

```
DescriptiveStatistics.cpp ×
        Source on Save    Q
  1  #include <Rcpp.h>
  2  |
  3  #include <string>
  4  #include <vector>
  5  #include <unordered_map>
  6
  7  #include "../../Common/include/Stats.h"
  8
  9  //' Retrieve descriptive statistics for a vector of values
 10  //'
 11  //' @param data A vector of doubles.
 12  //' @param keys An optional vector of keys.
 13  //' @export
 14  // [[Rcpp::export]]
 15  std::unordered_map<std::string, double>
 16 ·  get_descriptive_statistics(Rcpp::NumericVector data, Rcpp::CharacterVector keys = Rcpp::CharacterVector::create()) {
 17
 18    std::vector<double> _data = Rcpp::as<std::vector<double> >(data);
 19    std::vector<std::string> _keys = Rcpp::as<std::vector<std::string> >(keys);
 20
 21    std::unordered_map<std::string, double> results = Stats::GetDescriptiveStatistics(_data, _keys);
 22    return results;
 23 ·  }
```

Looking at Listing 6-1, there are a number of points that are worth highlighting:

- The include files: Here, we `#include` the main Rcpp header followed by the Standard Library includes. This is followed by the `#include` of `"Stats.h"`.

- The comment block: Here, we document the function parameters with their name and type. We also use the `@export` symbol to make the R wrapper function available to other R functions outside this package by adding it to the *NAMESPACE*. Don't confuse this with the `Rcpp::export` attribute that follows.

- Attributes: We mark the function `[[Rcpp::export]]`. This indicates that we want to make this C++ function available to R. We have already seen an example of this with the `library_version` function in the previous chapter.

- The wrapper function: Finally, the code itself – the R function is called `get_descriptive_statistics`. The first parameter is a `NumericVector`. The second parameter is an optional `CharacterVector`. If no argument is supplied, this is defaulted. The default argument is specified using the static `create` function. This allows us to retain the same calling semantics as the native C++ function. That is, we can call it with either one or two parameters. The `get_descriptive_statistics` function returns a `std::unordered_map<std::string, double>`, as does the underlying C++ function.

The code inside the `get_descriptive_statistics` function in Listing 6-1 is straightforward. We use the Rcpp function `as<T>(...)` to convert the incoming argument `NumericVector vec` (typedef'd as `Vector<REALSXP>`) from an SEXP (pointer to an S expression object) to a `std::vector<double>`. Similarly, we use `Rcpp::as<T>` to convert the `CharacterVector` keys to a vector of `strings`. We pass the parameters to the underlying C++ library function `GetDescriptiveStatistics` and retrieve the results. The results are then passed back to R using the native STL type. Under the hood, the results are wrapped as we describe in the following.

It should be clear from the preceding description that Rcpp allows us to write C++ code without being at all intrusive. Moreover, Rcpp facilitates the development process. Let's take a concrete example. If we wished to add functions to expose the underlying individual statistics, `ExcessKurtosis`, for example, this is a straightforward change. We need to include the descriptive statistics header file:

```
#include "../../Common/include/DescriptiveStatistics.h"
```

Next, we create a new function and mark it for export, as the following code shows:

```
//' Compute excess kurtosis
//'
//' @param data A vector of doubles.
//' @export
// [[Rcpp::export]]
double excess_kurtosis(Rcpp::NumericVector data) {

  std::vector<double> _data = Rcpp::as<std::vector<double> >(data);

  double result = Stats::DescriptiveStatistics::ExcessKurtosis(_data);
  return result;
}
```

This function takes a `NumericVector` and returns a `double`. The function uses `Rcpp::as<T>` to convert the `NumericVector` to a `std::vector<double>` and then calls the underlying library and returns the result. You might like to try adding this, rebuilding the package, and testing out the function interactively, as follows:

```
> StatsR::excess_kurtosis(c(0,1,2,3,4,5,6,7,8,9))
[1] -1.224242
```

As we have seen, when we invoke "Clean and Rebuild", the Rcpp framework updates the generated *src\RcppExports.cpp* file. It is instructive to look at the actual exported function generated in the file (but not to edit it). This is shown in Listing 6-2.

Listing 6-2. Rcpp generated code for the `get_descriptive_statistics` function

```
  9   std::unordered_map<std::string, double> get_descriptive_statistics(Rcpp::NumericVector data, Rcpp::CharacterVector keys);
 10 ▾ RcppExport SEXP _StatsR_get_descriptive_statistics(SEXP dataSEXP, SEXP keysSEXP) {
 11   BEGIN_RCPP
 12       Rcpp::RObject rcpp_result_gen;
 13       Rcpp::RNGScope rcpp_rngScope_gen;
 14       Rcpp::traits::input_parameter< Rcpp::NumericVector >::type data(dataSEXP);
 15       Rcpp::traits::input_parameter< Rcpp::CharacterVector >::type keys(keysSEXP);
 16       rcpp_result_gen = Rcpp::wrap(get_descriptive_statistics(data, keys));
 17       return rcpp_result_gen;
 18   END_RCPP
 19 ▾ }
```

Looking at the generated code in Listing 6-2, we can see how similar this is to the C++ function we have written. The function name is synthesized from the package name and the C++ name; hence, it is called "`_StatsR_get_descriptive_statistics`". This is declared with the `RcppExport` macro. This declares the function as `extern "C"`. Apart from this, the main differences between the wrapper C++ code we have written and the Rcpp generated C++ code center on the types used under the hood. Without getting bogged down in the details, Rcpp uses `SEXP` (S expression pointers) for incoming types. And it uses an `RObject` type for outgoing types. These are basically pointer types. `Rcpp::wrap` creates a new pointer with a copy of the returned object using one of the forms of `wrap_dispatch`, for example:

```
template <typename T> inline SEXP wrap_dispatch(const T& object,
::Rcpp::traits::wrap_type_module_object_tag) {
    return Rcpp::internal::make_new_object<T>(new T(object));
}
```

At the same time, it converts the type to an `RObject` and assigns the `RObject` pointer to `rcpp_result_gen`, which is then returned to R. The copy of the `std::unordered_map` that is returned from `GetDescriptiveStatistics` is destroyed, while the `RObject` contains a copy. It should be clear from this description that, at a slightly higher level, `Rcpp::wrap` provides RAII (Resource Acquisition is Initialization) around the (pointers to the) objects returned from our native C++ code. That is `Rcpp::wrap` provides lifetime management which simplifies the C++ wrapper code considerably.

You might be wondering how this is actually presented in an R session. From the R point of view, `std::unordered_map<std::string, double>` is returned as a numeric class, as the script in Listing 6-3 shows.

Listing 6-3. Retrieving the R class from a C++ wrapper function

```
# StatsR
stats <- StatsR::get_descriptive_statistics(data)
> class(stats)
[1] "numeric"
```

The numeric vector we return makes use of the Named class. The Named class is a helper class used for setting the key side of key/value pairs. The result is that calling get_ descriptive_statistics returns a numeric vector with labels, as shown in Listing 6-4.

Listing 6-4. Labelled output from the get_descriptive_statistics function

```
> stats <- StatsR::get_descriptive_statistics(c(0,1,2,3,4,5,6,7,8,9))
> stats
Variance.S        Sum      StdErr    StdDev.P       Skew.P        Mean
Count       Skew.S     Maximum  Variance.P     StdDev.S
 9.1666667 45.0000000   0.9574271  2.8722813   0.0000000  4.5000000
10.0000000   0.0000000   9.0000000  8.2500000   3.0276504
    Range    Kurtosis    Minimum      Median
 9.0000000 -1.2000000   0.0000000  4.5000000
```

We can transpose the output such that the named columns become rows, simply by coercing the returned NumericVector into a data frame as follows:

```
> stats <- as.data.frame(stats)
> stats
              stats
Variance.S  9.1666667
Sum         45.0000000
...
```

Exception Handling

Returning to the code generated in *RcppExports.cpp*, there is one detail that we skipped over: the macros BEGIN_RCPP/END_RCPP. These macros define try{...} catch{...} blocks to handle exceptions that might be thrown by the C++ code. The exception handling logic is quite involved. If you are interested, the macros are defined in *\Rcpp\include\Rcpp\macros\macros.h*. If the underlying C++ function throws a std::exception, it will be caught and translated appropriately. Listing 6-5 shows an example.

Listing 6-5. An example of exception handling

```
# StatsR
> stats <- StatsR::get_descriptive_statistics(c(1,2))
Error in StatsR::get_descriptive_statistics(c(1, 2)) : Insufficient data to
perform the operation.
```

From Listing 6-5, we can see that if we pass in too few data points to the underlying GetDescriptiveStatistics function, the exception is reported in an informative way. Summarizing what we have seen so far, it is clear that the Rcpp framework allows us to write clean C++ code while taking care of numerous details relating to translating between R and C++.

Exercising the Functionality

After doing a Clean and Rebuild, we can exercise the get_descriptive_statistics function and compare the results with the equivalent Base R functions. The script *DescriptiveStatistics.R* illustrates one way to do this. First, we load some additional packages: tidyverse and formattable, among others. The script then generates 1000 normally distributed random samples. Following this, we create two sets of data, one from *StatsR* and one using the equivalent *Base R* functions. We create a column to compare the results and add the three columns (*StatsR*, *BaseR*, and *Results*) to a data frame. The data frame is then formatted into a table. The row coloring changes depending on the TRUE/FALSE value in the results column, allowing us to easily detect differences in the results. These are shown in Figure 6-1.

	StatsR	BaseR	Equal
Skew	0.172508	0.172508	TRUE
Variance.S	1.040960	1.040960	TRUE
StdErr	0.032264	0.032264	TRUE
Sum	-7.255917	-7.255917	TRUE
Mean	-0.007256	-0.007256	TRUE
Maximum	3.574195	3.574195	TRUE
Count	1000.000000	1000.000000	TRUE
StdDev.S	1.020275	1.020275	TRUE
Minimum	-3.112947	-3.112947	TRUE
Range	6.687142	6.687142	TRUE
Kurtosis	3.070158	3.070158	TRUE
Median	0.002319	0.002319	TRUE

Figure 6-1. *Comparison of statistics: StatsR vs. BaseR*

From the table in Figure 6-1, we can immediately see that there are no numeric differences in the values produced by both libraries.

Linear Regression

The Code

The C++ code for exposing our simple univariate linear regression follows the same pattern as the descriptive statistics. This is shown in Listing 6-6.

Listing 6-6. Wrapper function for `LinearRegression`

```
LinearRegression.cpp ×
⇦⇨ | 🗐 | 🔲 □ Source on Save | 🔍 🛠 ▾
  8
  9  //` Perform simple univariate linear regression: y ~ x, (where y = B0 + xB1)
 10  //`
 11  //` @param xs A vector of doubles.
 12  //` @param ys A vector of doubles.
 13  //` @export
 14  // [[Rcpp::export]]
 15▾ std::unordered_map<std::string, double> linear_regression(Rcpp::NumericVector xs, Rcpp::NumericVector ys) {
 16
 17    std::vector<double> _xs = Rcpp::as<std::vector<double> >(xs);
 18    std::vector<double> _ys = Rcpp::as<std::vector<double> >(ys);
 19
 20    std::unordered_map<std::string, double> results = Stats::LinearRegression(_xs, _ys);
 21    return results;
 22▴ }
```

After the `#includes`, the function itself is declared as taking two `NumericVector`s and returning the results as before using `std::unordered_map<std::string, double>`. And as before, we use `Rcpp::as<T>` to copy the incoming vector to an STL type and rely on the implicit `wrap` to convert the results into a package of name value pairs. As discussed in the previous section, we leave the exception handling to the code generated by the Rcpp framework.

Exercising the Functionality

We'd like to test-drive this wrapper function, for example, by modelling some house price data and predicting a new price. The script *LinearRegression.R* shown in Listing 6-7 demonstrates one way to do this.

Listing 6-7. A simple linear model for house price prediction

```
LinearRegression.R ×

Source on Save

1   # Linear Regression
2   library(StatsR)
3   library(ggplot2)
4
5   predict <- function(b0, b1, x){
6     return (b0 + b1 * x)
7   }
8
9   data <- read.table(file.path(getwd(),'../data/HouseData.csv'),
10                      header=TRUE, sep=",",
11                      fileEncoding = "UTF-8-BOM")
12  ggplot(data, aes(x=Size, y=Price)) +
13    geom_point()+
14    geom_smooth(method=lm, se=FALSE)
15
16  results <- StatsR::linear_regression(data$Size, data$Price)
17  results
18  b0 <- results["b0"]
19  b1 <- results["b1"]
20
21  size = 2.5
22  predicted_price <- predict(b0, b1, size);
23  sprintf("Predicted price for size: %.2f sq ft= %.2fk",
24          size * 1000, predicted_price * 100)
25  fm <- lm(Price ~ Size, data=data)
26
27  # Fit a simple linear regression and look at the analysis.
28  summary(fm)
29  |
```

The script in Listing 6-7 begins by loading the StatsR library and ggplot2. We define a simple predict function that will use the results of the linear regression. Next, we load the data. This is the same data that we used in Chapter 4 (in *DataModelling.cs*). Next, we plot the data and add a regression line. This is shown in Figure 6-2.

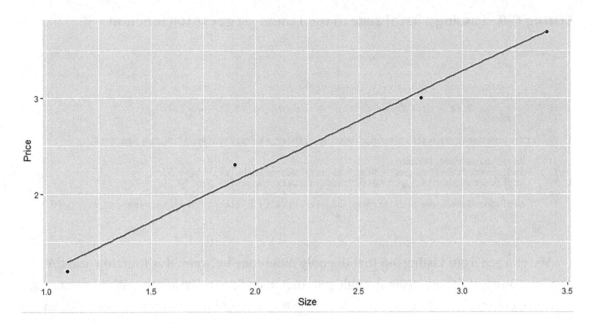

Figure 6-2. *Scatterplot of house price against size*

We call the wrapper function StatsR::linear_regression to obtain the model results and use the coefficients to predict a new value. Finally, we compare the results with the equivalent (but much more powerful) lm function in R. We can see that both the intercept (b0) and the slope (b1) are identical.

Using a DataFrame

From an R user's perspective, the linear_regression function might be improved by being able to call it with a DataFrame. We can rewrite the linear_regression function to do this as shown in Listing 6-8.

Listing 6-8. Passing a `DataFrame` to the `linear_regression` function

```
LinearRegression.cpp ×
      Source on Save   Q   
24   //' Perform simple univariate linear regression: y ~ x, (where y = B0 + xB1)
25   //'
26   //' @param data A data frame containing columns named 'x' and 'y'.
27   //' @export
28   // [[Rcpp::export]]
29   std::unordered_map<std::string, double> linear_regression(Rcpp::DataFrame data) {
30
31       Rcpp::DataFrame D(data);
32       std::vector<double> _xs = Rcpp::as<std::vector<double> >(D["x"]);
33       std::vector<double> _ys = Rcpp::as<std::vector<double> >(D["y"]);
34
35       std::unordered_map<std::string, double> results = Stats::LinearRegression(_xs, _ys);
36       return results;
37   }
```

We can see from Listing 6-8 that the only difference between this function and the previous one is that we pass in a single parameter, an `Rcpp::DataFrame`. We assume there are columns labelled "x" and "y". If the required column names do not exist, an error is generated:

("Error in StatsR::linear_regression(data) : Index out of bounds: [index='x'].").

We extract the columns as before into `std::vector<double>` types which we then pass to the C++ `LinearRegression` function. The results are returned as before. Calling the function now looks like this:

```
> data <- data.frame("x" = c(1.1, 1.9, 2.8, 3.4), "y" = c(1.2, 2.3, 3.0, 3.7))
> results <- StatsR::linear_regression(data)
> results
      b1         b0       SS_xy     x-mean      SS_xx     y-mean
1.0490196  0.1372549  3.2100000  2.3000000  3.0600000  2.5500000
```

The only caveat with this approach is that the compiler does not permit both `linear_regression` functions to exist. The error from the compiler is

"conflicting declaration of C function 'SEXPREC* _StatsR_linear_regression(SEXP)' ".

It appears not to be able to distinguish the one-parameter case from the two-parameter case. We can live with this by either insisting on a single function, or renaming one of the functions. The important point here is that in the wrapper layer, you can choose how to convert and present types to users.

Statistical Tests

Functions vs. Classes

The code for exposing the statistical tests functionality is located in *StatisticalTests.cpp*. We initially take the same approach to wrapping up the functionality as we have done previously in the StatsExcel component. That is, we wrap a C++ class in a procedural interface. Listing 6-9 shows part of the code.

Listing 6-9. Wrapper function to perform a t-test from summary data

```
StatisticalTests.cpp ×
            Source on Save    🔍  ✦  ▾
   7
   8   #include "../../Common/include/StatisticalTests.h"
   9
  10   //' Perform a t-test from summary input data
  11   //'
  12   //' @param mu0 Population mean.
  13   //' @param mean Sample mean.
  14   //' @param sd Sample standard deviation.
  15   //' @param n Sample size.
  16   //' @export
  17   // [[Rcpp::export]]
  18   std::unordered_map<std::string, double> t_test_summary_data(double mu0, double mean, double sd, double n) {
  19
  20       Stats::TTest test(mu0, mean, sd, n);
  21
  22       test.Perform();
  23       std::unordered_map<std::string, double> results = test.Results();
  24       return results;
  25   }
  26
```

The code in Listing 6-9 shows the function to perform a t-test from summary input data. The wrapper function takes four doubles as arguments (`double mu0, double mean, double sd, double n`) and returns the results as a package of key/value pairs. In the code, we need to construct a `Stats::TTest` object corresponding to the summary data t-test. We use the function arguments as parameters to the constructor. In the one-sample and two-sample cases, we pass in either one or two `NumericVector`s which are converted to a `std::vector<double>` as required. These are the same type of conversions that we have seen previously. After calling `test.Perform`, we obtain the results set. We could check explicitly if `Perform` returns `true` or `false`. However, if an exception is thrown, it will be handled by the Rcpp generated code.

Rcpp Modules

As we have seen, exposing existing C++ functions and classes to R through Rcpp is quite straightforward. The approach we have adopted until now is to write a wrapper function. This interface function is responsible for converting input objects to the appropriate types, calling the underlying C++ function, or constructing an instance if it is a class, and then converting the results back to a type suitable for R. We have seen a number of examples of both usages: exposing functions and classes with wrapper functions.

In certain circumstances however, it might be desirable to be able to expose classes directly to R. If the underlying C++ class has significant construction logic, for example. We would rather expose a class-like object that can be managed by R rather than incurring the cost of constructing an instance of the class on each function call, as we do with the t-test wrapper functions. More generally, exposing classes directly allows us to retain the underlying object semantics. The Rcpp framework provides a mechanism for exposing C++ classes via Rcpp modules. Rcpp modules also allow grouping of functions and classes in a single coherent modular unit.

To create a module, we use the RCPP_MODULE macro. Inside the macro, we declare the constructors, methods, and properties of the class we are exposing. Listing 6-10 shows how the TTest class can be exposed to R along with the declaration of the module.

Listing 6-10. Exposing the TTest class via the RCPP_MODULE macro

```
62
63  // A wrapper class for t-tests
64  class TTest
65 ▾ {
66  public:
67    ~TTest() = default;
68
69    TTest(double mu0, double mean, double sd, double n)
70      : _ttest(mu0, mean, sd, n)
71    {}
72
73    TTest(double mu0, Rcpp::NumericVector x1)
74      : _ttest(mu0, Rcpp::as<std::vector<double> >(x1))
75    {}
76
77    TTest(Rcpp::List data)
78      : _ttest(Rcpp::as<std::vector<double> >(data["x1"]), Rcpp::as<std::vector<double> >(data["x2"]))
79    {}
80
81    bool Perform()
82 ▾  {
83      return _ttest.Perform();
84 ▴  }
85
86    std::unordered_map<std::string, double> Results() const
87 ▾  {
88      std::unordered_map<std::string, double> results = _ttest.Results();
89      return results;
90 ▴  }
91
92  private:
93    Stats::TTest _ttest;
94 ▴ };
95
96
97 ▾ RCPP_MODULE(StatsTests) {
98
99    Rcpp::class_<TTest>("TTest")
100     .constructor<double, double, double, double>("Perform a t-test from summary input data")
101     .constructor<double, Rcpp::NumericVector >("Perform a one-sample t-test with known population mean")
102     .constructor<Rcpp::List>("Perform a two-sample t-test: args 'x1' and 'x2'")
103     .method("Perform", &TTest::Perform, "Perform the required test")
104     .method("Results", &TTest::Results, "Retrieve the test results")
105     ;
106
107 ▴ }
108
```

The code in Listing 6-10 is in *\src\StatisticalTests.cpp*. There are two parts to this code. The first part declares a C++ TTest wrapper class. This class wraps a native Stats::TTest member. The C++ wrapper class is used to perform the required translations between types. The constructors for the summary data and one-sample t-tests take the same Rcpp arguments as in the procedural wrappers and perform the same conversions we have seen before. The two-sample t-test uses an Rcpp::List object containing two numeric vectors labelled "x1" and "x2". The methods Perform and Results are simply forwarded to the underlying native Stats::TTest instance. The design pattern is similar to a pimpl (pointer-to-implementation) idiom or a facade or adaptor pattern.

The second part of the code declares the RCPP_MODULE macro. We define the class name as "*StatsTests*". This will be used by R to identify the module. Within the module, a class is exposed using the class_ keyword. The trailing underscore is required as we cannot use the C++ language keyword class. Here, class_<T> is templated by the C++ class or struct that is to be exposed to R, in this case, the name of our wrapper class. The string "*TTest*" that is passed into the class_<TTest> constructor is the name we will use when calling the class from R. Following this, we describe the class in terms of constructors, methods, and fields (not illustrated here). We can see that in this case, we have the three constructors corresponding to a summary data t-test, and both the one-sample and two-sample t-tests. The template arguments are the parameters of the respective underlying constructors. The use of Rcpp::List instead of two Rcpp::NumericVector parameters is a convenient way to package up the input arguments. It also provides a straightforward workaround to the issue that the RCPP_MODULE constructor method cannot distinguish between the following constructors:

```
.constructor<double, Rcpp::NumericVector>
.constructor<Rcpp::NumericVector, Rcpp::NumericVector>
```

Besides the constructors, in Listing 6-10, we can see that we have two methods. The method function takes the function name followed by the address of the wrapper function, followed by a help string. In general terms, we are providing a declarative description of the class to Rcpp. We also supply documentation strings. Listing 6-11 shows an example of how the TTest class can be used.

Listing 6-11. Using the TTest class in an R script

```
moduleStatsTests <- Module("StatsTests", PACKAGE="StatsR")
ttest0 <- new(moduleStatsTests$TTest, 5, 9.261460, 0.2278881e-01, 195)
if(ttest0$Perform()) {
  print(ttest0$Results())
} else {
  print("T-test from summary data failed.")
}
```

In Listing 6-11, we create a module object by calling the Module function with the name "StatsTests". Entities inside the module may be accessed via the $ symbol. Note that in our limited example, we have only placed a single entity inside the Rcpp module. However, there is no reason why this could not also contain other classes and related functionality. In R, we instantiate our TTest class as ttest0 using new with the object name followed by the parameters. We can then use the instance ttest0 to perform the test and print the results or an error message.

Overall, RcppModules provide a convenient way both to group functionality and to expose C++ classes. We therefore have the choice of writing wrapper functions or wrapper classes, whichever suits our purposes best. This has been a brief introduction to RcppModules. There are numerous details of this approach that we have not covered here.

Testing

Now that we have exposed the functionality of the underlying statistical library, it is useful to test that everything works as expected. For unit testing, we use the "*testthat*" library (https://testthat.r-lib.org/). The tests are organized in the *tests**testthat* directories under the main project. The *testthat.R* script under *tests* invokes the unit tests under *testthat*. There are three test files corresponding to the three areas of functionality:

- *test_descriptive_statistics.R*

- *test_linear_regression.R*

- *test_statistical_tests.R*

The tests follow the same *arrange-act-assert* form that we have used on previous occasions. In the case of both the descriptive statistics and linear regression tests, we check the results against Base R functions. Listing 6-12 shows an example for linear regression test.

Listing 6-12. The `LinearRegression` test

```
test_linear_regression.R ×
 1   context("Linear Regression")
 2
 3 ▾ test_that("Linear Regression values", {
 4
 5     x <- 1:20                                      # Make x = (1, 2, . . . , 20).
 6     w <- 1 + sqrt(x)/2                             # A 'weight' vector of standard deviations.
 7     y = x + rnorm(x)*w
 8
 9     dummy <- data.frame(x = x, y = y)              # Make a data frame of two columns, x and y
10     fm <- lm(y ~ x, data=dummy)                    # Fit a simple linear regression
11
12     results = StatsR::linear_regression(x, y)
13
14     expect_equal(fm$coefficients[["(Intercept)"]], results[["b0"]])
15     expect_equal(fm$coefficients[["x"]], results[["b1"]])
16
17 ▴ })
```

The `LinearRegression` test in Listing 6-12 creates x and y values and places these in a data frame. We then call the R function lm followed by our `LinearRegression` function. Finally, we compare the intercept and slope coefficients.

For the statistical hypothesis tests, we choose to test against hardcoded expected values (Listing 6-13).

Listing 6-13. Testing the summary t-test from data

```
test_statistical_tests.R ×
 1   context("Statistical Tests")
 2
 3 ▾ test_that("T-test from data", {
 4
 5     results = StatsR::t_test(5, 9.261460, 0.2278881e-01, 195)
 6
 7     expect_equal(2611.28380, results[["t"]])
 8     expect_equal(0.000e+000, results[["pval"]])
 9     expect_equal(194.0, results[["df"]])
10     expect_equal(9.26146, results[["x1-bar"]])
11     expect_equal(0.02278881, results[["sx1"]])
12     expect_equal(195.0, results[["n1"]])
13
14 ▴ })
```

In Listing 6-13, we only test the wrapper function as it is slightly easier to call than the class.

All the tests can be run by opening the *testthat.R* script and clicking the Source button. This is shown in Figure 6-3.

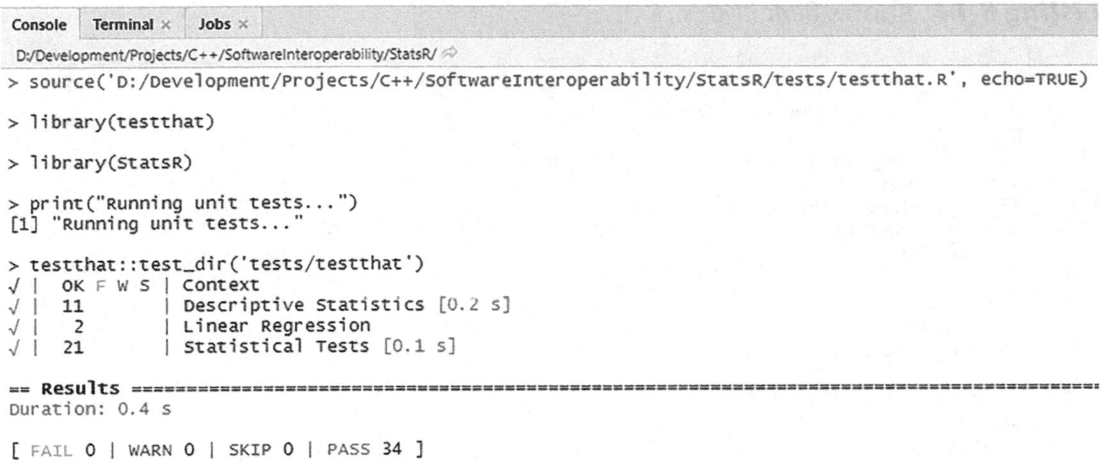

```
Console   Terminal ×   Jobs ×
D:/Development/Projects/C++/SoftwareInteroperability/StatsR/
> source('D:/Development/Projects/C++/SoftwareInteroperability/StatsR/tests/testthat.R', echo=TRUE)

> library(testthat)

> library(StatsR)

> print("Running unit tests...")
[1] "Running unit tests..."

> testthat::test_dir('tests/testthat')
√ |  OK F W S | Context
√ |  11       | Descriptive Statistics [0.2 s]
√ |   2       | Linear Regression
√ |  21       | Statistical Tests [0.1 s]

== Results ===================================================================================
Duration: 0.4 s

[ FAIL 0 | WARN 0 | SKIP 0 | PASS 34 ]
```

Figure 6-3. *Running the test harness*

The output from the test run in Figure 6-3 indicates that all the tests (34 of them) passed. There were no failures, warnings, or tests that were skipped. It also outputs the test durations.

Measuring Performance

One of the reasons for using C++ for lower-level code is the potential for performance gains when compared to using just R. Therefore, it seems worthwhile to try to measure this. Listing 6-14 shows *Benchmark.R*

Listing 6-14. shows *Benchmark.R*

```
 6 |
 7 library(tidyverse)
 8 library(bench)
 9 library(rbenchmark)
10 library(ggplot2)
11 library(StatsR)                              # Native C++ stats library
12
13 # Preliminaries
14 # Get the data
15 attach(mtcars)
16
17 mtcars <- as.data.frame(mtcars)
18 ggplot(mtcars, aes(x=wt, y=mpg)) +
19   ggtitle("Regression of MPG on Weight") +
20   geom_point() +
21   geom_smooth(method=lm)
22
23 ggplot(mtcars, aes(x=wt)) +
24   geom_density() +
25   geom_vline(aes(xintercept=get_descriptive_statistics(wt, "Mean")),
26             color="blue", linetype="dashed", size=1)
27
28 ggplot(mtcars, aes(x=mpg)) +
29   geom_density() +
30   geom_vline(aes(xintercept=get_descriptive_statistics(mpg, "Mean")),
31             color="blue", linetype="dashed", size=1)
32
33 # StatsR
34 StatsR <- function(x, y){
35   results = StatsR::linear_regression(x, y)
36   return
37 }
38
39 # R
40 R_LM <- function(df){
41   model <- lm(mpg ~ wt, data=df)
42   return
43 }
44
45 result <- bench::mark( StatsR(mtcars$wt, mtcars$mpg), R_LM(mtcars) )
46 result
47 plot(result)
48
```

The benchmark script in Listing 6-14 compares the performance of the C++ linear_ regression function with R's lm function. The comparison is somewhat artificial. R's lm function is far more flexible than our simple linear regression function. The comparison is for illustrative purposes only. The script loads a number of libraries, including the rbenchmark library. This is useful for micro-benchmarking functions. We use the well-known R dataset mtcars to perform a regression of mpg against weight. As usual, we plot the data beforehand and check the distributions using a density plot. We wrap the two functions that we are interested in comparing in dummy functions so that bench::mark does not complain that the result sets are different. Then we call bench::mark(...) with both functions. We output the result to the console.

```
                                    total_time
1 StatsR(mtcars$wt, mtcars$mpg)     178ms
2 R_LM(mtcars)                      491ms
```

The actual results are considerably more detailed than those shown earlier. However, we have summarized the total_time to illustrate the approach. We can see that the total_time taken by the *StatsR* function is 178ms compared to 491ms for the *R_LM* function. We also plot the output, shown in Figure 6-4.

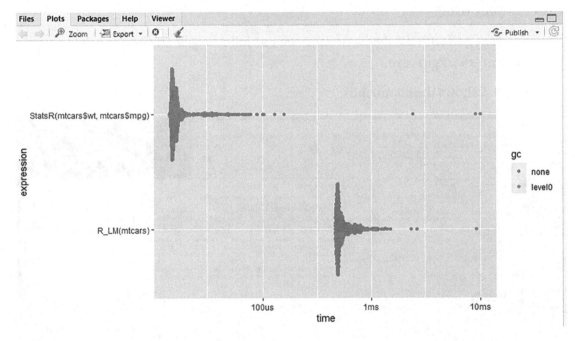

Figure 6-4. *Benchmark comparison of StatsR and R lm functions*

The difference in the timings is not surprising since the lm function does much more than our limited LinearRegression function.

Debugging

RStudio supports debugging of R functions in the IDE. Simply set the breakpoint(s) at appropriate locations and *Source* the file. Then, we can step through the R code line by line inspecting variables interactively and so on. Unfortunately, debugging the C++ code in a package is more difficult and less informative. It is possible to do this using *gdb*. However, for this we need to use Rgui as the host environment rather than RStudio. A full treatment of debugging R is beyond the scope of this chapter. However, should you need to, the process for attaching to the Rgui process and breaking into the debugger is as follows:

- Navigate to the directory with the sources (*\SoftwareInteroperability\ StatsR\src*).

- Start gdb with the Rgui as a parameter as follows: gdb D:/R/R-4.0.3/ bin/x64/Rgui.exe.

  Figure 6-5 shows the commands.

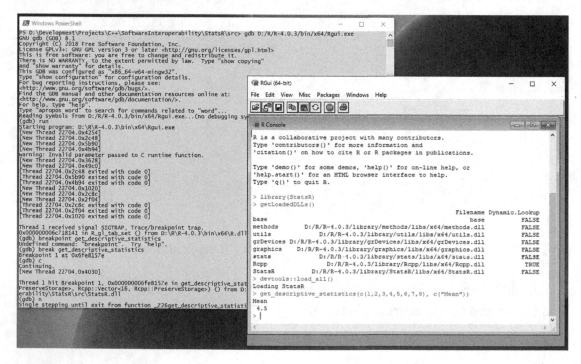

Figure 6-5. *A typical gdb session*

Note that we have interleaved the gdb session with the Rgui session. After starting gdb, type in run. This will run Rgui. See Figure 6-5. Then in Rgui, run devtools::load_all(). This will rebuild the *StatsR.dll* if necessary and will install and load the package. Next, in Rgui, select Misc ➤ Break to Debugger to return to the gdb session. In gdb, set the breakpoints you want. For example, we can set a breakpoint on get_descriptive_statistics. Use the command:

```
break get_descriptive_statistics
```

Then press c to return control to Rgui and continue. In Rgui, execute

```
> get_descriptive_statistics(c(1,2,3,4,5,6,7,8), c("Mean"))
```

This will now break into the debugger at the call location. From here we can single step through the function call (command n). However, the information from the individual function calls is quite limited, which makes debugging less useful than it should be.

Distribution Explorer

As pointed out in Chapter 4, when developing wrapper components, we are concerned not only with whether or not the functions (and classes) work correctly but also with how the component as a whole interoperates. With this in mind, the StatsR project contains a small Shiny App called Distribution Explorer. This is based on an existing example from the Shiny gallery (https://shiny.rstudio.com/gallery/) and adapted to use StatsR functionality. The user interface is shown in Figure 6-6.

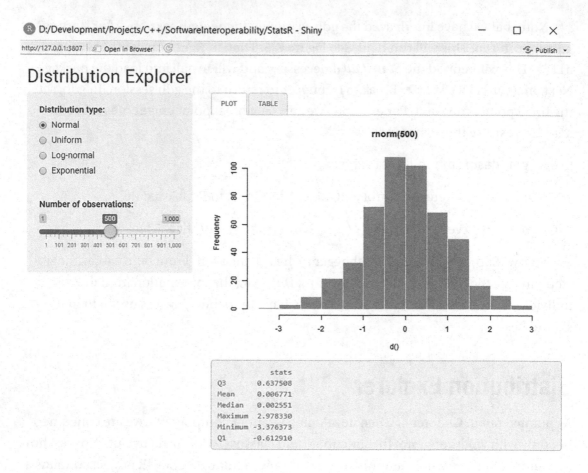

Figure 6-6. *StatsR Shiny App*

The Distribution Explorer generates a (configurable) number of random observations from the selected distribution in the left-hand panel. In the right-hand panel, it displays a histogram of the data and, more importantly from our point of view, produces summary statistics using the StatsR function get_descriptive statistics. Listing 6-15 shows the code.

Listing 6-15. Displaying summary statistics

```
84
85 ▾   # Generate a summary of the data ----
86 ▾   output$summary <- renderPrint({
87
88       data <- d()
89       stats <- StatsR::get_descriptive_statistics(data, c("Minimum", "Q1", "Median", "Mean", "Q3", "Maximum"))
90       stats <- as.data.frame(stats)
91       stats <- format(stats, scientific = FALSE, digits=4)
92       stats.table.df <- data.frame(stats)
93       names(stats.table.df)[1] <- "StatsR"
94       stats
95       #data
96 ▴   })
```

The summary statistics `stats` are rendered to a summary panel declared in the
UI `fluidPage`. Once the data has been generated, we extract it as a single column
`NumericVector`. This is passed to `get_descriptive_statistics` in the usual way along
with the keys representing the summary statistics we want returned. Presenting the
results takes a few more lines of code. First, we coerce the results into a `DataFrame` and
format the numeric values. Then we coerce the results into a table format and return
them. As can be seen, our StatsR package works, more or less seamlessly, with other R
packages.

Summary

In this chapter, we have written a fully functioning R package that connects to a native
C++ library. We have exposed both functions and classes from the underlying library
so that they are available for use in R/RStudio. We have tested the functionality and
benchmarked it.

Once we have these pieces in place (an RStudio Rcpp project, Rtools available for
compiling and building, and a C++ development environment), there is nothing to
stop us using any of the analytics offered in public domain C++ libraries as part of an
R data analysis toolchain. We might, for example, take QuantLib (`www.quantlib.org/`)
and use some of the interest rate curve building functionality in R. Alternatively, we
might consider developing our own C++ libraries, and making these available in R. It is
worth emphasizing that this goes beyond the more traditional use-case of writing small
amounts of C++ code that are compiled and run inline in R with a view to improving
performance. These two chapters have provided a working infrastructure for more
systematic development of C++ components with the intention of making

the functionality available in an R package. Rcpp makes this process seamless and takes away much of the work involved. In the next two chapters, we look at a similar situation, but in this case, our focus is on the Python language and Python clients.

Additional Resources

The following links go into more depth on the topics covered in this chapter:

- Rcpp is a large library. For a user-friendly introduction, I would recommend "Rcpp for everyone" at `https://teuder.github.io/rcpp4everyone_en/`. The official package documentation is available here: `https://cran.r-project.org/web/packages/Rcpp/Rcpp.pdf`. However, depending on what type of information you are looking for, there are various other sources. Apart from the book "Seamless R and C++ Integration with Rcpp" (see the References), there is a good amount of documentation covering all aspects of the package at `https://github.com/RcppCore/Rcpp`. Particularly recommended are the vignettes which focus on specific features of Rcpp (like RcppModules, for example). I would also recommend the Rcpp FAQ at `https://cran.r-project.org/web/packages/Rcpp/vignettes/Rcpp-FAQ.pdf`.

Exercises

The exercises in this section deal with incorporating the various changes we have made to the underlying codebase into the R package, and exposing the functionality via Rcpp. All the exercises use the StatsR RStudio project.

1) We extended the `LinearRegression` function to calculate the correlation coefficient r and r^2 and added these to the results package. Confirm that the additional coefficients calculated in the `LinearRegression` function are displayed, and check the values.

For this, you can use the script *LinearRegression.R*. To check the results, use the functions `cor(data)` and `cor(data)^2`. Compare these values to the values obtained in the results package from the function `StatsR::linear_regression(...)`. The results should be identical.

Extend the test case in *test_linear_regression.R* to include a check of these values.

2)   The `TimeSeries` class has already been added to the sources, and built into the *libStatsLib.a* static library (see Chapter 5). Expose the `MovingAverage` function from the `TimeSeries` class. In this case, we just want to expose a procedural wrapper function. In a further exercise, we will add a class using RcppModules.

The steps required are as follows:

- In the *\src* directory add a new file *TimeSeries.cpp*. Use File ➤ New ➤ C++ File as this will create the file with the boilerplate Rcpp code.

- #include the *TimeSeries.h* file from the *\Common\include* directory.

- Expose the `MovingAverage` method using a procedural wrapper. The following function signature is suggested:

  ```
  std::vector<double> get_moving_average(Rcpp::NumericVector dates,
  Rcpp::NumericVector observations, int window) { ... }
  ```

- Implement the code:

  - Convert the dates to a vector of `long`s.

  - Convert the observations to a vector of `double`s.

  - Construct an instance of the `TimeSeries` class.

  - Call the `MovingAverage` function and return the results.

- Select Build ➤ Clean and Rebuild and check that the build (still) works without warnings or errors. Check that the file *\src\TimeSeries.cpp* compiled correctly in the output. Check that the function is present in *RcppExports.R*.

- Check that the function is present in the list of functions. Use

  ```
  > library(pkgload)
  > names(pkg_env("StatsR"))
  ```

3)   Add an R script *TimeSeries.R* to exercise the new function.

- Create some random data as follows:

  ```
  n = 100                        # n samples
  observations <- 1:n + rnorm(n = n, mean = 0, sd = 10)
  dates <- c(1:n)
  ```

- Add a simple moving average function with a default window size of 5:

```
moving_average <- function(x, n = 5) {
    stats::filter(x, rep(1 / n, n), sides = 1)
}
```

- Obtain two moving averages: one from the StatsR package and one using the local function (note the window size parameter):

```
my_moving_average_1 <- StatsR::get_moving_average(dates,
observations, 5)
my_moving_average_2 <- moving_average(observations, 5)
# Apply user-defined function
```

- Plot the series.

- Compare the series as they should be identical:

```
equal <- (my_moving_average_1 - my_moving_average_2)
>= (tolerance - 0.5)
length(equal[TRUE])
```

4)   Add procedural wrappers for the three z-test functions. These should be similar to the t-test wrappers, that is:

```
z_test_summary_data(...)
z_test_one_sample(...)
z_test_two_sample(...)
```

- Select Build ➤ Clean and Rebuild and check that the build works without warnings or errors. Check that the file \src\StatisticalTests.cpp compiled correctly in the output. Check that the functions are present in RcppExports.R. Check that the functions are present in the list of functions.

- Use the R script StatisticalTests.R to write a script to exercise the new functions. The following script uses the same data as is used in the native C++ unit tests, the C# unit tests, and the Excel worksheet:

```
#
# z-tests
#

# Summary data z-test
StatsR::z_test_summary_data(5, 6.7, 7.1, 29)

# One-sample z-test data
StatsR::z_test_one_sample(3, c(3, 7, 11, 0, 7, 0, 4, 5, 6, 2))

# Two-sample z-test data
x <- c( 7.8, 6.6, 6.5, 7.4, 7.3, 7.0, 6.4, 7.1, 6.7, 7.6, 6.8 )
y <- c( 4.5, 5.4, 6.1, 6.1, 5.4, 5.0, 4.1, 5.5 )

StatsR::z_test_two_sample(x, y)
```

- For completeness, add test cases to \testthat\test_statistical_tests.R.

- Run the *testthat.R* script and confirm that all the tests pass.

5) Under the StatsR project, in the *man* directory, there is an R markdown document named *StatsR-package.Rd*. Update the document with the new functions: get_moving_average, z_test_summary_data, z_test_one_sample, and z_test_two_sample.

- Select Preview to view the changes. Select Build ➤ Clean and Rebuild. Check the file: *"D:\R\R-4.0.3\library\StatsR\html\StatsR-package.html"*.

6) Add the ZTest as a class to the RcppModule StatsTests.

- In *StatisticalTests.cpp*, write a wrapper class that contains a private member variable:

```
Stats::ZTest _ztest;
```

- Implement the conversions required in the constructors. This is basically identical to the TTest wrapper.

- Add this class to the RcppModule:

```
...
{
Rcpp::class_<ZTest>("ZTest")
.constructor<double, double, double, double>("Perform a z-test
from summary input data")
.constructor<double, Rcpp::NumericVector >("Perform a one-sample
z-test with known population mean")
.constructor<Rcpp::List >("Perform a two-sample z-test")
.method("Perform", &ZTest::Perform, "Perform the required test")
.method("Results", &ZTest::Results, "Retrieve the test results")
  ;
}
```

- In RStudio, select Build ➤ Clean and Rebuild and check that the build works without warnings or errors. Check that the file \src\ *StatisticalTests.cpp* compiled correctly in the output.

- Use the R script *StatisticalTests.R* to write a script to exercise the new class. The following is an example of the summary data z-test:

```
library(Rcpp)
library(formattable)

moduleStatsTests <- Module("StatsTests", PACKAGE="StatsR")
ztest0 <- new(moduleStatsTests$ZTest, 5, 6.7, 7.1, 29)
if(ztest0$Perform())
{
  results <- ztest0$Results()
  print(results)
  results <- as.data.frame(results)
  formattable(results)
}
else
{
  print("Z-test from summary data failed.")
}
```

7)   Add the `TimeSeries` as a class to a new RcppModule.

- Open *TimeSeries.cpp* source file.

- Add a wrapper class for the native C++ time series as follows:

```
// A wrapper class for time series
class TimeSeries
{
public:
  ~TimeSeries() = default;

  TimeSeries(Rcpp::NumericVector dates, Rcpp::NumericVector
  observations)
    : _ts(Rcpp::as<std::vector<long> >(dates),
    Rcpp::as<std::vector<double> >(observations) )
  {}

  std::vector<double> MovingAverage(int window) {
    return _ts.MovingAverage(window);
  }

private:
  Stats::TimeSeries _ts;
};
```

- Define an `RCPP_MODULE(TS)` that describes the wrapper class, for example:

```
Rcpp::class_<TimeSeries>("TimeSeries")
  .constructor<Rcpp::NumericVector, Rcpp::NumericVector>("Construct
  a time series object")
  .method("MovingAverage", &TimeSeries::MovingAverage, "Calculate
  a moving average of size = window")
  ;
```

- Select Build ➤ Clean and Rebuild and check that the build works without warnings or errors.

- Open the file *TimeSeries.R*. Add code to the script that computes the same time series as previously and compares the results.

```
moduleTS <- Module("TS", PACKAGE="StatsR")
ts <- new(moduleTS$TimeSeries, dates, observations)
my_moving_average_4 <- ts$MovingAverage(5)
equal <- (my_moving_average_4 - my_moving_average_2) >=
(tolerance - 0.5)
length(equal[TRUE])
```

PART IV

Python

## CHAPTER 7

Building a Python Extension Module

Introduction

In this chapter and the next, we look at building Python extension modules. These are components that connect C/C++ to Python. Python has been around for quite some time, and over the years, a number of different approaches to accomplishing this have been developed. Table 7-1 lists some of the approaches.

Table 7-1. *Approaches to connecting C/C++ to Python[1]*

Approach	Vintage	Representative users
C/C++ extension modules for CPython	1991	Standard Library
PyBind11 (recommended for C++)	2015	
Cython (recommended for C)	2007	gevent, kivy
HPy	2019	
mypyc	2017	
ctypes	2003	oscrypto
cffi	2013	cryptography, pypy
SWIG	1996	crfsuite
Boost.Python	2002	
cppyy	2017	

[1] Source: https://docs.microsoft.com/en-us/visualstudio/python/
working-with-c-cpp-python-in-visual-studio?view=vs-2019.

© Adam Gladstone 2022
A. Gladstone, *C++ Software Interoperability for Windows Programmers*,
https://doi.org/10.1007/978-1-4842-7966-3_7

In this chapter and the following, we focus on three main approaches. These are highlighted in Table 7-1. In this chapter, we start off with a "raw" Python project using CPython. This is instructive. We get to see how to set up a Python extension module project from scratch and how to expose the functionality from our small statistical library. It gives us a chance to see how modules are defined, and how the `PyObject` is used in the translation layer. It also illustrates some of the difficulties of a low-level approach. Chapter 8 focuses on Boost.Python and then PyBind. Both these frameworks offer useful facilities that overcome some of the issues we face when writing a CPython extension module. We also look at how to expose classes as well as functions. Finally, we use the modules we have built to illustrate inspecting objects and measuring performance among other things.

Prerequisites

For this chapter and the next, the main prerequisite is a Python installation (`www.python.org/downloads/`). For this book, we have used Python 3.8 (the latest available when this project was started). Apart from the version of Python, we need to be aware of the build environment. In the next chapter, we will need Boost.Python and the Boost.Python library needs to be built against this same version of Python.

Using Visual Studio Community Edition 2019

It is perfectly possible to use Visual Studio to manage both the C++ projects (which we do) and the Python projects (which we do not) in the same solution. This has the advantage that you can debug Python scripts in the same environment that you develop your C++ components. However, this setup has a downside. It ties us to the version of Python that the Visual Studio Community Edition 2019 targets (currently Python 3.7). And this in turn produces an undesirable misalignment of versions of Python, Boost.Python, and the C++ projects. To develop Python modules, we really need to line up versions of Python (3.8) and the Boost library's distribution of Boost.Python (built using Python 3.8).

As a result, the recommendation here is to separate the two areas of development. We use Visual Studio Community Edition 2019 for the C++ wrapper components and VSCode for the Python project and scripts. This means we get the convenience of compiling the extension module using MSBuild as opposed to having to write our own setup and build script. This approach has the advantage of making debugging somewhat easier though not quite as seamless as using fully mixed-mode debugging.

StatsPythonRaw

Our first extension module is a "raw" Python project called StatsPythonRaw. We look first at the project setup, and then at how the code is organized. Within this, we examine how the functions from the underlying statistics library can be exposed and the type conversion layer. We also deal with exception handling. In the final section, we exercise the functionality from a Python client and look at debugging the extension module.

Project Settings

StatsPythonRaw is created as a Windows Dynamic-Link Library (DLL) project. The project references the StatsLib static library. The project settings are summarized in Table 7-2.

Table 7-2.   Project settings for StatsPythonRaw

Tab	Property	Value
General	C++ language Standard	ISO C++17 Standard (/std:c++17)
Advanced	Target File Extension	*.pyd*
C/C++ > General	Additional Include Directories	*<Users\user>\Anaconda3\include* *$(SolutionDir)Common\include*
Linker > General	Additional Library Directories	*<Users\user>\Anaconda3\libs*
Build Events > Post-Build Event	Command Line	See in the following

It is worth noting the following points. Firstly, we change the target output from *dll* to *pyd*. This indicates that the output is a Python extension library. Secondly, we need to note where the Python installation is located. In the additional include directories, we reference the *include* directory where *Python.h* can be found. In the additional library directories, we reference the *libs* directory (not *Lib* or *Library* which are also present in the Python distribution). This is where *python38.lib* can be found. Lastly, we copy the *StatsPythonRaw.pyd* module to the directory where the Python script (**.py*) which imports it is located. We use the following script in the post-build step:

```
del "$(SolutionDir)StatsPython\$(TargetName).pyd"
copy /Y "$(OutDir)$(TargetName)$(TargetExt)" "$(SolutionDir)StatsPython\$(
TargetName)$(TargetExt)"
```

This simplifies the Python setup. By copying the *pyd* file to the location where the script will be executed, we avoid having to call *setup.py* to install the Python module into the Python environment. In a production scenario, this would be required. However, for the purposes of ease of exposition we take this shortcut.

Code Organization

Under the StatsPythonRaw project, the code is organized into three main areas: the functions we want to expose (*Functions.h/Functions.cpp*), the conversion layer (*Conversion.h/Conversion.cpp*), and the extension module that we are building (*module. cpp*). We will deal with each of these in turn.

Functions

Declarations

In the file *Functions.h*, we declare the wrapper functions that we use to expose the underlying functionality. For convenience, we have located all the functions under a single namespace called API. Listing 7-1 reproduces the complete declaration.

Listing 7-1. Declaration of the wrapper functions we want to expose

```
Functions.h  ⌐ ×
StatsPythonRaw              ▾       (Global Scope)                                     ▾
     1      #pragma once
     2
     3      #define PY_SSIZE_T_CLEAN
     4    ⊟//
     5     | // Prevent linking against pythonXY_d.lib
     6     | //
     7    ⊟#ifdef _DEBUG
     8     | #undef _DEBUG
     9     | #include <Python.h>
    10     | #define _DEBUG
    11    ⊟#else
    12     | #include <Python.h>
    13      #endif
    14
    15    ⊟namespace API
    16     | {
    17     |      // Retrieve a package of descriptive statistics for the input data
    18     |      PyObject* DescriptiveStatistics(PyObject* /* unused module reference */, PyObject* args);
    19     |
    20     |      // Perform simple univariate linear regression: y ~ x, (where y = B0 + xB1)
    21     |      PyObject* LinearRegression(PyObject* /* unused module reference */, PyObject* args);
    22     |
    23     |      // Wrapper function for a t-test with summary input data (no sample)
    24     |      PyObject* SummaryDataTTest(PyObject* /* unused module reference */, PyObject* args);
    25     |
    26     |      // Wrapper function for a one-sample t-test with known population mean
    27     |      PyObject* OneSampleTTest(PyObject* /* unused module reference */, PyObject* args);
    28     |
    29     |      // Wrapper function for a two-sample t-test
    30     |      PyObject* TwoSampleTTest(PyObject* /* unused module reference */, PyObject* args);
    31     | }
```

In Listing 7-1, the preprocessor macros at the top of the file are important. The Python documentation (see the Additional resources section) recommends that we use #define PY_SSIZE_T_CLEAN before including any standard library headers. The macro refers to the type of the size variable when using sized objects, lists, and arrays, for example. If the macro is defined, then the size-type is Py_ssize_t, otherwise the size-type is int. Following this, we have some build directives. We want to be able to build a debug and release version of this extension module. However, we do not want to link against the debug version of the Python libraries as we have not installed them. Without this preprocessor directive, when we build a debug version of StatsPythonRaw, the linker will attempt to link against *python38_d.lib*. As we do not have this, it produces a build error. So, we are required to UNDEF'ine the _DEBUG symbol. If you download and install the Python debug libraries, you can remove this. Lastly, #include <Python.h> pulls in the Python API.

Inside the API namespace, all of the C++ wrapper functions return a PyObject pointer. This can be thought of as an opaque type or a handle. In general, the Python runtime passes us parameters as PyObjects, which we then need to interpret. When we return from functions, we need to return PyObjects to the Python runtime. Specifically, from Listing 7-1 we can see that the wrapper functions always take two PyObject parameters, conventionally named self and args. The self parameter points to the module object for module-level functions (as would be the case here); for a class method, it points to the object instance (i.e., the object invoking the call). We do not use this argument in this project, so we ignore it. For the args parameter, we distinguish two cases. In the case of a function with a single argument, this is passed directly in the Python object. In the case of a function with multiple arguments, the args parameter points to a tuple object. Each item of the tuple corresponds to an argument in the parameter list of the call. We will deal with how the tuple is interpreted later in the chapter.

Descriptive Statistics

Having looked at the function declarations, we now look at the function definitions. We start off with the simplest function that we want to expose. In the underlying C++ library, the function GetDescriptiveStatistics (in *\StatsLib\Stats.h*) is declared as taking two parameters, the second of these is optional. We want to call this function from Python as shown in Listing 7-2.

Listing 7-2. Calling the DescriptiveStatistics function from Python

```
>>> import StatsPythonRaw as Stats
>>> data = [0, 1, 2, 3, 4, 5, 6, 7, 8, 9]
>>> results = Stats.DescriptiveStatistics(data)
>>> print(results)
{'Mean': 4.5, 'Count': 10.0, 'Kurtosis': 1.7757575757575756, 'Kurtosis.XS': -1.2242424242424244, 'Maxim
um': 9.0, 'Minimum': 0.0, 'Q1': 2.25, 'Median': 4.5, 'Q3': 6.75, 'Range': 9.0, 'Skew': 0.0, 'StdDev.P':
 2.8722813232690143, 'StdDev.S': 3.0276503540974917, 'StdErr': 0.9574271077563381, 'Sum': 45.0, 'Varian
ce.P': 8.25, 'Variance.S': 9.166666666666666}
>>> keys = ['Mean', 'StdDev.P']
>>> results = Stats.DescriptiveStatistics(data, keys)
>>> print(results)
{'Mean': 4.5, 'StdDev.P': 2.8722813232690143}
>>> █
```

From Listing 7-2, the interactive Python session, we can see that we call the function first with a single argument (data) and then with two arguments (data, keys). Listing 7-3 shows the corresponding C++ wrapper function definition.

Listing 7-3. The definition of the `DescriptiveStatistics` function

```
Functions.cpp  ⊕  ×  Functions.h
StatsPythonRaw              ▾  ⟨⟩ API                                          ▾  ● DescriptiveStatistics(PyObject *, PyObject * args)
   18        {
   19     ⊞    // ...
   22     ⊟    PyObject* DescriptiveStatistics(PyObject* /* unused module reference */, PyObject* args)
   23        {
   24            STATS_TRY
   25
   26            PyObject* data = nullptr;
   27            PyObject* keys = nullptr;
   28
   29     ⊟        if (!PyArg_ParseTuple(args, "O|O", &data, &keys)) {
   30                return nullptr;
   31            }
   32
   33            std::vector<double> _data = Conversion::ObjectToVector(data);
   34            std::vector<std::string> _keys = Conversion::ObjectToStringVector(keys);
   35
   36            std::unordered_map<std::string, double> results = Stats::GetDescriptiveStatistics(_data, _keys);
   37            return Conversion::MapToObject(results);
   38            STATS_CATCH
   39        }
```

The structure of the function is straightforward. The first part concerns extracting
the PyObject pointers from the args tuple. The second part consists of translating these
for the underlying C++ layer and returning the results. The function PyArg_ParseTuple
in the Python API checks the argument types and converts them to C/C++ values. It uses
a template string to determine the required types of the arguments as well as the types
of the C/C++ variables into which to store the converted values. The template string
determines how the tuple unpacks its arguments. In this case, we tell it that there are two
PyObject pointers, this is indicated by the "O" (uppercase letter). The "|" separating the
"O|O" string indicates that the second argument is optional. Later, we will see some more
examples of using the template string. The following list summarizes some of the more
common argument types used in the template string.

String	Conversion
"i"	Convert a Python integer to an int.
"l"	Convert a Python integer to a long.
"d"	Convert a Python floating point number to a double.
"O"	Store a Python object in a PyObject pointer.

A full list of the argument types and their usage in template strings is given here:
https://docs.python.org/3/c-api/arg.html.

In this case, as we have said, both the arguments are Python objects. In order to do anything with them, our function has to convert them to C/C++ types. Here, the first argument is converted to a `std::vector<double>` using the function `ObjectToVector`. Similarly, we convert the second argument from a `PyObject` to a `std::vector<std::string>` using `ObjectToStringVector`. The converted objects (`_data`, `_keys`) are passed to the native C++ function, and the results are returned packaged as key-value pairs in a `std::unordered_map`. These are then converted back to a pointer to a `PyObject` and returned to the caller.

Linear Regression

Before going on to look in more detail at the conversion functions, we take a look at more of the functions that we want to we expose. Listing 7-4 shows the wrapper function for `LinearRegression`.

Listing 7-4. The wrapper function for `LinearRegression`

```
Functions.cpp  ⊅  ×  Functions.h
StatsPythonRaw                    ▾  {} API                                                ▾  ◉ LinearRegression(PyObject *, PyObject * args)
  41  ⊞      // ...
  44  ⊟      PyObject* LinearRegression(PyObject* /* unused module reference */, PyObject* args)
  45         {
  46             STATS_TRY
  47             PyObject* xs = nullptr;
  48             PyObject* ys = nullptr;
  49
  50  ⊟          if (!PyArg_ParseTuple(args, "OO", &xs, &ys)) {
  51                 return nullptr;
  52             }
  53
  54             std::vector<double> _xs = Conversion::ObjectToVector(xs);
  55             std::vector<double> _ys = Conversion::ObjectToVector(ys);
  56             std::unordered_map<std::string, double> results = Stats::LinearRegression(_xs, _ys);
  57             return Conversion::MapToObject(results);
  58             STATS_CATCH
  59         }
```

We can see in Listing 7-4 that this function follows a similar structure to the `DescriptiveStatistics` function we looked at previously. In this case, however, the `args` parameter contains two non-optional items. Hence, the template string is `"OO"`. These represent the two datasets required to perform the operation. Before we can call the native C++ function, we need to unpack the `args` tuple into valid `PyObjects`, `xs` and `ys`. Then we need to convert each of the items to an appropriate C++ type. Once this is done, we call the underlying C++ function and return the results.

Statistical Tests

For the statistical test functions, we structure the functions in the same way as previously. However, in this case, the wrapper function creates an instance of the TTest class on the stack. For this, it needs to pass the arguments into the corresponding constructors. An example of this is shown in Listing 7-5.

Listing 7-5. The SummaryDataTTest wrapper function

```
Functions.cpp  ⊕ ×  Functions.h
StatsPythonRaw            ▾ () API                                             ▾  ● SummaryDataTTest(PyObject *, PyObject * args)
   61    ⊞     // ...
   64    ⊟   PyObject* SummaryDataTTest(PyObject* /* unused module reference */, PyObject* args)
   65        {
   66            STATS_TRY
   67            double mu0{ 0.0 };
   68            double mean{ 0.0 };
   69            double sd{ 0.0 };
   70            double n{ 0.0 };
   71
   72    ⊟       if (!PyArg_ParseTuple(args, "dddd", &mu0, &mean, &sd, &n)) {
   73                return nullptr;
   74            }
   75
   76            Stats::TTest test(mu0, mean, sd, n);
   77            test.Perform();
   78
   79            const auto results = test.Results();
   80            return Conversion::MapToObject(results);
   81            STATS_CATCH
   82        }
```

Up to now, we have seen the PyObject* args tuple being passed into PyArg_ParseTuple and the arguments extracted as PyObjects. However, in Listing 7-5, we take advantage of the standard conversions. The t-test from sample data constructor requires four doubles. We therefore unpack the args tuple using PyArg_ParseTuple with the template string "dddd" to represent the four doubles. Because these are built-in types, the function PyArg_ParseTuple converts these implicitly. No further conversion is required. The function then proceeds to create the TTest instance and call Perform to do the calculation followed by Results to obtain the results package. This is then converted back to a Python dictionary.

Both the OneSampleTTest and TwoSampleTTest are handled in a similar way. The OneSampleTTest is shown in Listing 7-6.

Listing 7-6. The OneSampleTTest wrapper function

```
Functions.cpp  ⊕ ×  Functions.h
StatsPythonRaw           ▼ {} API                                              ▼  ● OneSampleTTest(PyObject *, PyObject * args)
    84    ⊞        // ...
    87    ⊟        PyObject* OneSampleTTest(PyObject* /* unused module reference */, PyObject* args)
    88            {
    89                STATS_TRY
    90                double mu0{ 0.0 };
    91                PyObject* o = nullptr;
    92
    93    ⊟            if (!PyArg_ParseTuple(args, "dO", &mu0, &o)) {
    94                    return nullptr;
    95                }
    96
    97                std::vector<double> data = Conversion::ObjectToVector(o);
    98
    99                Stats::TTest test(mu0, data);
   100                test.Perform();
   101
   102                const auto results = test.Results();
   103                return Conversion::MapToObject(results);
   104                STATS_CATCH
   105            }
```

From Listing 7-6 and the previous listings we can see the similar structure of both the functions OneSampleTTest and TwoSampleTTest. We first declare the types we are expecting from the args. Then we use PyArg_ParseTuple with the appropriate template string to unpack the arguments into either built-in types or PyObject pointers. Then we do any further conversion that is required before returning the results to Python. In the case of the OneSampleTTest, the template string is "dO", indicating that the first parameter is a double and the second parameter is a PyObject. Hence, we use a standard conversion for the first argument (double mu0) and unpack the second argument to a PyObject pointer, which is then converted to a std::vector<double> as we have seen previously.

The Conversion Layer

We have already seen that for built-in types (bool, int, double, etc.), we don't need to do anything special. The conversion is handled by PyArg_ParseTuple with the appropriate template string argument. For the STL types, the conversion layer (*Conversion.h/ Conversion.cpp*) provides a central location for the type conversion logic. There are only three functions. One to convert a PyObject representing a Python list to a std::vector<double>. The second function is to convert a PyObject representing a Python list of strings into a std::vector<std::string>. Lastly, we have a function to convert our results (an unordered map of string keys and numeric values) into a PyObject pointer. Listing 7-7 shows the ObjectToVector function.

Listing 7-7. Converting a PyObject to a std::vector<double>

```
Conversion.cpp  ╪  ×   Conversion.h

StatsPythonRaw            ▾  ⟨⟩ Conversion              ▾  ● ObjectToVector(PyObject * o)
    12    ⊞       // ...
    15    ⊟       std::vector<double> ObjectToVector(PyObject* o)
    16            {
    17                std::size_t size = PyList_Size(o);
    18                std::vector<double> data;
    19
    20    ⊟           for (std::size_t i = 0; i < size; ++i)
    21                {
    22                    double d = PyFloat_AsDouble(PyList_GetItem(o, i));
    23                    data.emplace_back(d);
    24                }
    25                return data;
    26            }
```

Looking at the code in Listing 7-7, we see that the conversion from a Python object to an STL type is straightforward. We are expecting the argument from Python to be a list, so we need to use the PyList_xxx functions. First, we get the size of the input list and then we use a for-loop to extract each item. We use the function PyList_GetItem to retrieve the indexed data item, and we convert this from a Python number to a double (PyFloat_AsDouble) as required. This is then placed into a std::vector<double>. When the loop completes, the data is returned to the caller.

Listing 7-8 shows the second of the three functions, ObjectToStringVector.

Listing 7-8. The `ObjectToStringVector` function

```
Conversion.cpp  ⊕ ×   Conversion.h
StatsPythonRaw            ▾  () Conversion                                            ▾  ● ObjectToStringVector(PyObject * o)
   28   ⊕       // ...
   31   ⊟       std::vector<std::string> ObjectToStringVector(PyObject* o)
   32           {
   33               std::vector<std::string> strings;
   34   ⊟           if (o != nullptr)
   35               {
   36                   std::size_t size = PyList_Size(o);
   37   ⊟               for (std::size_t i = 0; i < size; ++i)
   38                   {
   39   ⊕                   // ...
   44                       std::string s((char*)PyUnicode_1BYTE_DATA(PyList_GetItem(o, i)));
   45                       strings.emplace_back(s);
   46                   }
   47               }
   48               return strings;
   49           }
```

The `ObjectToStringVector` function shown in Listing 7-8 converts a Python list to a vector of strings. We can see that this is similar to the previous function. In this case, we first check that the input object is valid. We know that the `PyObject` here represents an optional parameter, so it is possible that the argument is null. In the previous case, the function `PyArg_ParseTuple` would fail if the argument were not supplied, so the check would be redundant. However, we should be aware that if we extend the usage of the `ObjectToVector` function (specifically allowing optional data), then we would need to change this. After the check, we proceed to extract the valid `PyObject` from the list. The difference in this case is that we need to convert it to a string. To keep things simple, we do not check if the Python string is Unicode UTF-8 or UTF-16. We simply assume UTF-8 and use the Python function `PyUnicode_1BYTE_DATA` to convert the string to a `char*`, which we then use in the constructor of the `std::string`. A more robust way to perform the conversion would be to check the various possible Python types and handle the cases accordingly. Handling strings in a generic fashion and which will work in a cross-platform environment is a surprisingly large topic and beyond the scope of this chapter.

Listing 7-9 shows the final function, `MapToObject`, which converts the results map to a Python dictionary.

Listing 7-9. Converting the underlying results package to a Python dictionary

```
Conversion.cpp  ⊕ ✕  Conversion.h
StatsPythonRaw            ▼  () Conversion                          ▼  ● MapToObject(const st(

    51  ⊞      // ...
    54  ⊟      PyObject* MapToObject(const std::unordered_map<std::string, double>& results)
    55         {
    56             PyObject* dict = PyDict_New();
    57
    58  ⊟         for (const auto& result : results)
    59             {
    60                 PyObject* key = PyUnicode_FromString(result.first.c_str());
    61                 PyObject* val = PyFloat_FromDouble(result.second);
    62
    63                 int success = PyDict_SetItem(dict, key, val);
    64                 Py_XDECREF(key);
    65                 Py_XDECREF(val);
    66  ⊟             if (success < 0)
    67                 {
    68                     Py_XDECREF(dict);
    69                     return nullptr;
    70                 }
    71             }
    72             return dict;
    73         }
    74  }
```

As we can see in Listing 7-9, the `MapToObject` function is slightly more involved than previously. In this case, we take as input a `const` reference to the results map. The first thing the code does is to create a new Python dictionary. Then we iterate over the result items and insert each item in the dictionary. The keys are strings so we use `PyUnicode_FromString` to perform the conversion. To obtain the value, we use `PyFloat_FromDouble` (as we have done before). Finally, we set the key-value pair that we have extracted as a dictionary item, and check if this has been successful. In this case, we need to decrement the reference counts for both the key and the value as we are no longer using the `PyObject` references. We use the `Py_XDECREF` macro, which allows the object to be null, rather than `Py_DECREF`. If `PyDict_SetItem` has not succeeded, we also need to decrement the reference count for the dictionary and return `nullptr` to indicate failure to the Python runtime.

Reference counting in this context is quite involved, but it is required in order to avoid memory leaks from Python. However, a full discussion of reference counting is beyond the scope of this chapter. The Python documentation contains a useful section on this topic.

It is clear by now that the conversion layer could be made more generic and thereby improved. Our three conversion functions are completely specific to the requirements of the underlying native C++ layer. It would be nice to be able to generalize some of the code. In particular, using RAII (Resource Acquisition is Initialization) to manage the reference counting seems like a useful approach. Additionally, handling default arguments and converting to and from the Standard Library containers with templates is also beneficial. While it might be tempting, writing a "general" conversion layer between C++ and Python can be tricky to get right and time-consuming to implement. The section on Additional resources gives a number of references on these topics. Fortunately, as we will see in the next chapter, both Boost.Python and PyBind do an excellent job in this regard.

Error Handling

We know that StatsLib throws exceptions. If we do not handle these, there is a possibility that from a Python script, we just terminate the Python shell. This is not necessarily what we want. So, as on previous occasions, we wrap our function call using STATS_TRY/ STATS_CATCH macros with code that translates the std::exception to an informational string that can be interpreted by Python.

The STATS_TRY/STATS_CATCH macros are defined as shown in Listing 7-10.

Listing 7-10. Handling exceptions

```
Conversion.cpp        Conversion.h  ⌗ ✕
StatsPythonRaw              ▾     (Global Scope)
    19
    20      #define STATS_TRY try{
    21
    22      #define STATS_CATCH \
    23  ⊟        }catch(const std::exception& e){  \
    24                PyErr_SetString(PyExc_RuntimeError, e.what());\
    25                return nullptr;\
    26            }
```

In Listing 7-10, after an exception has been thrown, we first indicate an error condition using the PyErr_SetString function. According to the documentation, Py_ DECREF is not required for objects passed to this function (https://docs.python.org/3/ extending/extending.html#refcounts). The first parameter is a Python exception object and the second is the informational string from the C++ function. The second stage is to indicate failure by returning `nullptr`. If we wish to take this further, we could create a standard exception for this module or we could extend the exception handling with a custom class. However, a full treatment of the topic of exception handling is beyond the scope of this chapter. The Additional resources section provides some more references.

Now that we handle exceptions in the C++ layer, we can add equivalent exception handling to our Python script. For example, we wrap the `DescriptiveStatistics` function in a `try/except` block and report any exceptions. After reporting the exception, code execution continues as normal. Listing 7-11 shows the code.

Listing 7-11. Reporting exceptions from Python

```
18    def report_exception(e: Exception) -> None:
19        """ Print out details of the exception """
20        print(type(e))      # the exception instance
21        print(e.args)       # arguments stored in .args
22
23
24    def run_descriptive_statistics(data: list) -> None:
25        """ Run descriptive statistics """
26        try:
27            summary: dict = Stats.DescriptiveStatistics(data)
28            print(summary)
29        except Exception as inst:
30            report_exception(inst)
31
```

The code in Listing 7-11 is straightforward. We take the exception thrown by the wrapper function and output the informational string. A typical interactive session shows how this appears:

```
>>> import StatsPythonRaw as Stats
>>> data = []
>>> print(Stats.DescriptiveStatistics(data))
Traceback (most recent call last):
  File "<stdin>", line 1, in <module>
RuntimeError: Insufficient data to perform the operation.
```

As we can see, we catch and report the C++ exception and return it to Python, where we can continue the interactive session.

The Module Definition

So far, we have covered calling functions and type conversions. The final piece we need for our Python extension module component is the module definition. The code is located in *module.cpp*. The code consists of three main sections: the exported functions, the module definition, and the initialization function. We will look at each of these in turn. Listing 7-12 shows the exported functions.

Listing 7-12. Exporting functions from the module

```
module.cpp  ⊣ ×
StatsPythonRaw          ▼   (Global Scope)                          ▼
    20    ⊞  // ...
    23       static PyMethodDef StatsPythonRaw_methods[] =
    24    ⊟  {
    25    ⊞      // ...
    28    ⊟      {
    29              "DescriptiveStatistics",
    30              (PyCFunction)API::DescriptiveStatistics,
    31              METH_VARARGS,
    32              "Retrieve a package of descriptive statistics for the input data."
    33          },
    34
    35    ⊟      {
    36              "LinearRegression",
    37              (PyCFunction)API::LinearRegression,
    38              METH_VARARGS,
    39              "Perform simple univariate linear regression: y ~ x, (where y = B0 + xB1)."
    40          },
    41
    42    ⊞      { ... },
    48
    49    ⊞      { ... },
    55
    56    ⊞      { ... },
    62
    63          // Terminate the array with an object containing nulls.
    64          { nullptr, nullptr, 0, nullptr }
    65      };
```

The exported functions (Listing 7-12) are defined in a `struct` which contains an array of the functions we want to export. The parameters are straightforward. The first parameter is the name of the function that is exposed to Python. The second parameter is the function that implements it. The function must conform to the `typedef`:

```
typedef PyObject *(*PyCFunction)(PyObject *, PyObject *)
```

This declares a function that takes two `PyObject` pointers as parameters and returns a `PyObject` pointer. This corresponds to how we have declared our functions (see Listing 7-1). The third parameter is a combination of `METH_xxx` flags which describe the `args` expected by the function. For a single argument function, we would use `METH_O`. This means the function takes a single `PyObject` argument. Functions that take `METH_O` are passed the `PyObject` directly in the `args` parameter. So, there is no need to use `PyArg_ParseTuple`. `METH_VARARGS` indicates that the function takes a variable number of arguments which will need to be unpacked by `PyArg_ParseTuple`. The final parameter is the Python docstring attribute (`__doc__`) or it can be a `nullptr`.

The list of exported functions is followed by the module definition structure, shown in Listing 7-13.

Listing 7-13. The module definition structure

```cpp
module.cpp  ⌐P  ✕
StatsPythonRaw              ▼    (Global Scope)                        ▼
66
67    ⊟static PyModuleDef StatsPythonRaw_module = {
68          PyModuleDef_HEAD_INIT,
69          "StatsPythonRaw",                  // Module name to use with Python import statements
70          "Python C++ StatsLib wrapper",     // Module description
71          0,
72          StatsPythonRaw_methods             // Structure that defines the methods of the module
73    };
74
75    ⊟PyMODINIT_FUNC PyInit_StatsPythonRaw()
76     {
77          return PyModule_Create(&StatsPythonRaw_module);
78     }
79
```

The PyModuleDef structure shown in Listing 7-13 defines the structure of the module. We initialize the structure with the symbol PyModuleDef_HEAD_INIT. Following this, we supply the module name to use with Python import statements, followed by a module description. The last parameter we use is a pointer to the structure that defines the exported methods (the structure defined in Listing 7-12). Following the module definition, we define the function PyInit_StatsPythonRaw with the name of our module. It is important that this matches the declared name in the module definition (i.e., *"StatsPythonRaw"*). The Python runtime environment will look for this function to call in order to perform the initialization of this module when it is being imported. That is it for this component. We can now build it. It should build without warnings or errors. The output file (*StatsPythonRaw.pyd*) will be copied into the StatsPython project, where we can import it in a Python script.

Python Client

Now that we have a working Python extension module which wraps native C++ functions, we can use it in any way we choose. We could launch a Jupyter notebook and make use of our functions as part of another project. Or as a quick test of the functions that we have exposed, we can also run Python's shell and use the read-evaluate-print loop (REPL) interactively. Listing 7-14 shows a small example.

Listing 7-14. Performing a summary data t-test

```
>>> import StatsPythonRaw as Stats
>>> results: dict = Stats.SummaryDataTTest(5, 9.26146, 0.22788e-01, 195)
>>> print(results)
{'t': 2611.3766182604695, 'pval': 0.0, 'df': 194.0, 'x1-bar': 9.26146, 'sx1': 0.022788, 'n1': 195.0}
```

As we can see from Listing 7-14, this provides a simple way to exercise the functions. As a slightly more sophisticated alternative, we can use the script *StatsPythonRaw.py*. This provides a more extensive test of the functions. The script defines a main function so we can run it directly from the command prompt (> python StatsPythonRaw.py). We can also open this directly in Visual Studio Code, for example, and execute it (F5). The main function is shown in Listing 7-15.

Listing 7-15. The main function exercising StatsPythonRaw

```python
87    if __name__ == "__main__":
88        """ Define standard data sets used elsewhere """
89        xs: list = [0, 1, 2, 3, 4, 5, 6, 7, 8, 9]
90        ys: list = [1, 3, 2, 5, 7, 8, 8, 9, 10, 12]
91
92        run_descriptive_statistics(xs)
93        run_linear_regression(xs, ys)
94
95        ttest_summary_data()
96
97        filename: str = "../Data/weight.txt"
98
99        # Read in data frame
100       df: pd.DataFrame = pd.read_csv(filename)
101
102       one_sample_ttest(df)
103
104       us_df: pd.DataFrame = pd.read_csv("../Data/us-mpg.txt")
105       jp_df: pd.DataFrame = pd.read_csv("../Data/jp-mpg.txt")
106
107       plot_data(us_df, jp_df)
108
109       two_sample_ttest(us_df, jp_df)
```

The script in Listing 7-15 defines the xs and ys datasets that we have used elsewhere. We use these as inputs to the descriptive statistics and linear regression functions. Next, we call the ttest_summary_data function. The final part of the code uses Pandas to load data into a data frame. Using this data, we perform a one-sample t-test. Finally, we load the *us-mpg* and *jp-mpg* datasets. These are the same datasets as we used in the StatsViewer MFC application. We use matplotlib to visualize the difference in the means in a boxplot (Figure 7-1), after which we perform a two-sample t-test.

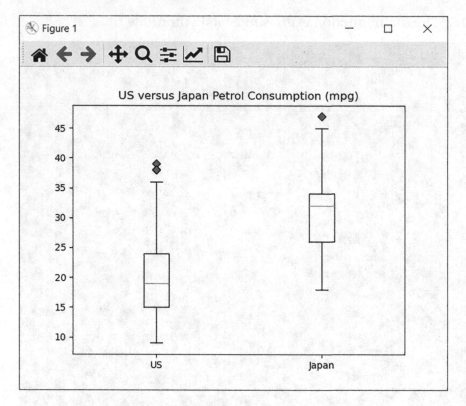

Figure 7-1. *Boxplot comparing US and Japanese car petrol consumption*

Debugging

Debugging both Python and C++ is surprisingly straightforward. Python debugging is handled well by the VSCode IDE. Debugging the C++ code is simply a matter of putting a breakpoint in the Python script in VSCode (Python execution will halt there) and then using Visual Studio (Debug ➤ Attach to Process...) to attach to the correct Python hosting process (you can use *procexp64.exe* to identify this easily). Then the script will jump into the C++ code, breaking at the appropriate locations (assuming you are calling into the debug version of the C++ module). From here you can step through the C++ code. This is only one of a number of possibilities. The Additional resources section provides some more details.

Summary

In this chapter, we have built a basic Python module from scratch. We first exposed functions from the underlying StatsLib and then we converted the types as required. Finally, we defined the module. This can be thought of as a declarative description (metadata) of the functions and parameters that we are exposing. In terms of consuming the Python module, we created a simple script. In addition to exercising some of the functionality, we also demonstrated how the module interoperates with Pandas and matplotlib.

As we pointed out in the introduction to this chapter, writing a module using "raw" CPython is instructive because it illustrates some of the difficulties involved in using a low-level approach to connecting C/C++ to Python. We have had to write specific code to handle the conversions that we required. Moreover, we have seen that we need to be aware of reference counting whenever we interact with `PyObjects`. In the next chapter, we look at the Boost.Python and PyBind frameworks and see how both of these ease the difficulties we have seen here.

Additional Resources

The following resources are useful for more information on the topics covered in this chapter:

- For all things related to Python, the excellent Python documentation can be found at `https://docs.python.org/3/`. Of particular interest for writing extension modules is the section on extending Python with C or C++. This is recommended: `https://docs.python.org/3/extending/extending.html`. For further information about building and installing Python modules, see `https://docs.python.org/3/extending/building.html#building` and `https://docs.python.org/3/extending/windows.html#building-on-windows`.

- The following document provides invaluable information on a wide range of topics related to Python extension modules: `https://pythonextensionpatterns.readthedocs.io/_/downloads/en/latest/pdf/`. In addition, it covers a robust approach to converting strings from Python to `std::string`.

- Approaches to generalizing the type conversion layer and providing robust lifetime management are discussed here: https:// pythonextensionpatterns.readthedocs.io/en/latest/cpp_and_ cpython.html. Examples of additional approaches can be found at https://github.com/mfontanini/Programs-Scripts/blob/ master/pywrapper/pywrapper.h and https://github.com/dubzzz/ Py2Cpp/blob/master/src/py2cpp.hpp.

- In terms of exception handling, the approach of creating a standard exception type for a module is described here: https:// docs.python.org/3/extending/extending.html. Extending the exception handling with a custom class is described here: https://pythonextensionpatterns.readthedocs.io/en/latest/ exceptions.html.

- Debugging mixed-mode C/C++ Python code in Visual Studio is described here: https://docs.microsoft.com/en-us/ visualstudio/python/debugging-mixed-mode-c-cpp-python-in- visual-studio?view=vs-2019.

Exercises

The exercises in this section deal with exposing the new C++ functionality to Python via our CPython extension module.

1)   Add procedural wrappers for the z-test functions. These should be almost identical to the t-test functions. No additional conversion functions are required so you can adapt the t-test functions in a straightforward way.

- In *Functions.h,* add declarations for the three functions:

```
// Wrapper function for a z-test with summary input data
(no sample)
PyObject* SummaryDataZTest(PyObject* /* unused module
reference */, PyObject* args);
```

```
// Wrapper function for a one-sample z-test with known
population mean
PyObject* OneSampleZTest(PyObject* /* unused module
reference */, PyObject* args);

// Wrapper function for a two-sample z-test
PyObject* TwoSampleZTest(PyObject* /* unused module
reference */, PyObject* args);
```

- In *Functions.cpp*, add the implementations of these functions. Follow the code for the t-test wrapper functions.

- In *module.cpp*, add the three new functions to the array:

```
static PyMethodDef StatsPythonRaw_methods[] =
{
//...
}
```

- Build StatsPythonRaw. It should build without warnings and errors. The functions should now be callable from Python. Try out the functions interactively, for example:

```
>>> import StatsPythonRaw as Stats
>>> results: dict = Stats.SummaryDataZTest(5, 6.7, 7.1, 29)
>>> print(results)
{'z': 1.2894056580462898, 'sx1': 7.1, 'pval':
0.19725709541241007, 'x1-bar': 6.7, 'n1': 29.0}
```

- Open the StatsPython project in VSCode. Open the *StatsPythonRaw. py* script. Add functions to test the z-test functions using the data we have used previously.

2)   Add a procedural wrapper function to calculate a simple MovingAverage. We know from previous exercises that we need to add some conversion functions when dealing with the time series moving average function. Specifically, in this Python case, we need to convert a PyObject to a vector of longs. Furthermore, we need to convert the results from std::vector<double> to a Python list.

The steps required to add the conversion functions are as follows:

- In *Conversion.h,* add the declaration for a conversion function:

```
std::vector<long> ObjectToLongVector(PyObject* o);
```

- In *Conversion.cpp,* add the implementation. This is similar to ObjectToVector, but it uses PyLong_AsLong to extract the long value from the PyObject.

  Similarly, we need to convert the results (a vector of doubles) into a Python list.

- In *Conversion.h,* add the declaration:

```
PyObject* VectorToObject(const std::vector<double>& results);
```

- In *Conversion.cpp,* add the following implementation:

```
PyObject* VectorToObject(const std::vector<double>& results)
{
    const std::size_t size = results.size();
    PyObject* list = PyList_New(size);

    for(std::size_t i = 0; i < size; ++i)
    {
        double d = results[i];
        int success = PyList_SetItem(list, i,
        Py_BuildValue("d", d));
        if (success < 0)
        {
            Py_XDECREF(list);
            return nullptr;
        }
    }
    return list;
}
```

- In this case, we create a new Python `list` using the input vector size. In order to set the list items, we use the function `PyList_SetItem`. We pass it the `PyObject` returned from the convenience function `Py_BuildValue` using a template string of `"d"` (for `double`).

With the conversion functions in place, write the wrapper function. The steps required to write the wrapper function are as follows:

- In *Functions.h,* add a declaration:

  ```
  PyObject* MovingAverage(PyObject* /* unused module reference
  */, PyObject* args);
  ```

- In *Functions.cpp*, there are a number of details:

  - Add `#include "TimeSeries.h"` to the top of the file.

  - Add the implementation. The function takes three non-optional arguments. A list of dates, a list of observations and a window size.

  - Add exception handlers `STATS_TRY`/`STATS_CATCH`.

  - Declare the input parameters:

    ```
    PyObject* dates = nullptr;

    PyObject* observations = nullptr;

    long window{ 0 };
    ```

  - Parse the input `args` with the template string `"OOl"`.

  - Convert the inputs as before to construct a time series.

  - Return the results using the `VectorToObject` conversion function.

- Finally, in *module.cpp,* add the new function to the list of exposed functions:

```
{
    "MovingAverage",
    (PyCFunction)API::MovingAverage,
    METH_VARARGS,
    "Compute a simple moving average of size = window."
},
```

- That completes the code for adding a procedural wrapper for the MovingAverage function.

- Build StatsPythonRaw. It should build without warnings and errors.

- Try out the function interactively, for example:

```
>>> import StatsPythonRaw as Stats
>>> dates: list = list(range(1, 16))
>>> observations: list = [1, 3, 5, 7, 8, 18, 4, 1, 4, 3, 5,
7, 5, 6, 7]
>>> sma: list = Stats.MovingAverage(dates, observations, 3)
>>> print(sma)
```

- Open the StatsPython project in VSCode. Open the *StatsPythonRaw. py script.* Add a function to test the moving average, including exception handling. Run the script, and debug if required.

## CHAPTER 8

Module Development with Boost.Python and PyBind

Introduction

In the previous chapter, we saw how to create a basic Python extension module. We added code to expose functionality from the underlying C++ library of statistical functions. We saw how to perform the conversion between PyObject pointers and native C++ types. While not especially difficult, we saw that it is potentially error prone. In this chapter, we consider two frameworks – Boost.Python and PyBind – that overcome these difficulties, making the development of Python extension modules easier. We build two quite similar wrapper components, the first based on Boost.Python and the second on PyBind. The intention here is to compare the two frameworks. Following this, we look at a typical Python client and develop a script to measure the relative performance of the extension modules. We end the chapter with a simple Flask app that demonstrates using our PyBind module as part of a (limited) statistics service.

Boost.Python

The Boost Python Library is a framework for connecting Python to C++. It allows us to expose C++ classes, functions, and objects to Python in a non-intrusive way using types provided by the framework. We can continue to write "regular" C++ code in the wrapper layer using the types provided. The Boost Python Library is extensive. It provides support

© Adam Gladstone 2022
A. Gladstone, *C++ Software Interoperability for Windows Programmers*,
https://doi.org/10.1007/978-1-4842-7966-3_8

for automatic conversion of Python types to Boost types, function overloading, and exception translation, among other things. Using Boost.Python allows us to manipulate Python objects easily in C++, simplifying the syntax when compared to a lower-level approach such as the one we saw in the previous chapter.

Prerequisites

In addition to an installation of Boost (we use Boost 1.76 for this project), we require a built version of the libraries. Specifically, we need the Boost Python library. Boost.Python is not a header-only library unlike most of the Boost library functionality, so we need to build it. Moreover, we need to ensure that when we build the libraries, the version of the Boost.Python library is consistent with the version of Python we are targeting. We have been using Python 3.8, so we expect the following Boost libraries to be present:

- *\boost_1_76_0\stage\lib\libboost_python38-vc142-mt-gd-x32-1_76.lib*

- *\boost_1_76_0\stage\lib\libboost_python38-vc142-mt-x32-1_76.lib*

- *\boost_1_76_0\stage\lib\libboost_python38-vc142-mt-gd-x64-1_76.lib*

- *\boost_1_76_0\stage\lib\libboost_python38-vc142-mt-x64-1_76.lib*

The Boost installation and build process for these libraries are described in more detail in Appendix A.

Project Settings

The StatsPythonBoost project is a standard Windows DLL project. As before, the project references the StatsLib static library. The project settings are summarized in Table 8-1.

Table 8-1. *Project settings for StatsPythonBoost*

Tab	Property	Value
General	C++ Language Standard	ISO C++17 Standard (/std:c++17)
C/C++ > General	Additional Include Directories	*<Users\user>\Anaconda3\include*
		$(BOOST_ROOT)
		$(SolutionDir)Common\include
Linker > General	Additional Library Directories	*<Users\user>\Anaconda3\libs*
		$(BOOST_ROOT)\stage\lib
Build Events > Post-Build Event	Command Line	(see in the following)

We can see from Table 8-1 that the project settings are similar to the previous project. In this case, we have not renamed the target output. We leave this for the post-build script (see in the following). In the Additional Include Directories, we reference the location of *Python.h* and the StatsLib project include directory. In addition, we reference the Boost libraries with $(BOOST_ROOT) macro. Similarly, in the Additional Library Directories, we add a reference to both the Python libs and the Boost libs.

As in the previous project, we take a shortcut. Rather than installing the library in the Python environment, we simply copy the output to our Python project location (*\StatsPython*). From there we can import the library in a Python script or interactively. In the post-build event, we copy the *dll* to the script directory, delete the previous version, and rename the *dll* with a *.pyd* extension, as follows:

```
copy /Y "$(OutDir)$(TargetName)$(TargetExt)" "$(SolutionDir)StatsPython\$(T
argetName)$(TargetExt)"
del "$(SolutionDir)StatsPython\$(TargetName).pyd"
ren "$(SolutionDir)StatsPython\$(TargetName)$(TargetExt)"
"$(TargetName).pyd"
```

With these settings in place, everything should build without warnings or errors.

Code Organization

The Visual Studio Community Edition 2019–generated project for a Windows *dll* generates a handful of files that we ignore. We ignore the *dllmain.cpp* file (which contains the entry point for a standard Windows *dll*). We also ignore the files *framework.h* and *pch.cpp* (except insofar as it includes *pch.h*, the precompiled header).

In the *pch.h* file, we have

```
#define BOOST_PYTHON_STATIC_LIB
#include <boost/python.hpp>
```

The macro indicates that in this *dll* module, we are statically linking to Boost Python:

\boost_1_76_0\stage\lib\libboost_python38-vc142-mt-...-...-1_76.lib

The *"..."* depend on the specific processor architecture, though in our case we target only x64. The second line brings in all the Boost Python headers. The rest of the code is organized as before into three main areas: the functions (*Functions.h/Functions.cpp*), the conversion layer (*Conversion.h/Conversion.cpp*), and the module definition. In addition, for this project, we have a wrapper class *StatisticalTests.h/StatisticalTests.cpp* that wraps up the t-test functionality. We will deal with each of these areas in turn.

Functions

Inside the API namespace we declare two functions: `DescriptiveStatistics` and `LinearRegression`. Both functions take the corresponding `boost::python` arguments. Boost.Python comes with a set of derived object types corresponding to those of Python's:

Python type	*Boost type*
• `list`	`boost::python::list`
• `dict`	`boost::python::dict`
• `tuple`	`boost::python::tuple`
• `str`	`boost::python::str`

This makes converting to STL types quite straightforward, as we shall see. The code inside the functions is also straightforward. We first convert the parameters to types usable by the StatsLib. Then we call the underlying C++ function, collect the results, and translate these back into a form Python understands. The Boost.Python library makes this very straightforward and flexible. Listing 8-1 shows the implementation of the `DescriptiveStatistics` function.

Listing 8-1. The `DescriptiveStatistics` wrapper function

```
Functions.cpp  ⌐ ×
StatsPythonBoost          ▼ {} API                      ▼ ● DescriptiveStatistics(const boost::python::list & data, const boost::python::list & keys)
   13   ⊞     // ...
   16   │     boost::python::dict DescriptiveStatistics(const boost::python::list& data,
   17   ⊟         const boost::python::list& keys /* = boost::python::list() */)
   18         {
   19             std::vector<double> _data = Conversion::to_std_vector<double>(data);
   20             std::vector<std::string> _keys = Conversion::to_std_vector<std::string>(keys);
   21
   22             const auto _results = Stats::GetDescriptiveStatistics(_data, _keys);
   23             boost::python::dict results;
   24             Conversion::to_dict(_results, results);
   25             return results;
   26         }
```

The `DescriptiveStatistics` function in Listing 8-1 should look familiar. It follows the same structure as the raw Python example in the previous chapter. The major difference in the function declaration is that instead of `PyObject` pointers, we can use types defined in the Boost.Python library. In this case, both parameters are passed in as `const` references to a `boost::python::list`. The second parameter is defaulted, as we want to be able to call `DescriptiveStatistics` with or without the keys. The input arguments are converted to a `std::vector<double>` and a `std::vector<std::string>`, respectively. These are then used in the call to the underlying statistical library function. The results package is returned as before (a `std::unordered_map<std::string, double>` type) and converted to a `boost::python::dict`.

Listing 8-2 shows the code for the `LinearRegression` function.

Listing 8-2. The `LinearRegression` wrapper function

```
Functions.cpp  ⌐ ×
StatsPythonBoost          ▼ {} API                      ▼ ● DescriptiveStatistics(const boost::python::list & data, const boost::python::list & keys)
   28   ⊞     // ...
   31   ⊟     boost::python::dict LinearRegression(const boost::python::list& xs, const boost::python::list& ys)
   32         {
   33             std::vector<double> _xs = Conversion::to_std_vector<double>(xs);
   34             std::vector<double> _ys = Conversion::to_std_vector<double>(ys);
   35
   36             const auto _results = Stats::LinearRegression(_xs, _ys);
   37             boost::python::dict results;
   38             Conversion::to_dict(_results, results);
   39             return results;
   40         }
   41
   42   }
```

As can be seen from Listing 8-2, the LinearRegression function follows the same structure as previously. The function takes in two lists, converts them into the corresponding datasets, calls the underlying function, and converts the results package into a Python dictionary.

StatisticalTests

Inside the API namespace, we create a separate namespace StatisticalTests for the three statistical hypothesis test functions. As in the "raw" case, here we have initially chosen to wrap up the usage of the TTest class inside a function. Listing 8-3 shows the summary data t-test function.

Listing 8-3. Wrapping up the TTest class in a function

```
StatisticalTests.cpp  ⊣ ×
StatsPythonBoost              ▼  ⟨⟩ API::StatisticalTests        ▼  ● SummaryDataTTest(const boost::p

    12                //
    13          |     boost::python::dict SummaryDataTTest(
    14                    const boost::python::object& mu0,
    15                    const boost::python::object& mean,
    16                    const boost::python::object& sd,
    17                    const boost::python::object& n
    18      ⊟     )
    19          {
    20                double _mu0 = boost::python::extract<double>(mu0);
    21                double _mean = boost::python::extract<double>(mean);
    22                double _sd = boost::python::extract<double>(sd);
    23                double _n = boost::python::extract<double>(n);
    24
    25                Stats::TTest test(_mu0, _mean, _sd, _n);
    26                test.Perform();
    27
    28                const auto _results = test.Results();
    29                boost::python::dict results;
    30                Conversion::to_dict(_results, results);
    31                return results;
    32          }
```

As shown in Listing 8-3, the approach of providing a procedural wrapper for a class is straightforward: we get the input data and create an instance of the TTest class (depending on the function call and the arguments). We then call Perform to do the calculation and Results to retrieve the results. These are then translated back to the Python caller. The SummaryDataTTest function in this example takes four parameters corresponding to the constructor arguments of the summary data t-test. The arguments are typed as const references to a boost::python::object. This provides a wrapper around PyObject. The function then makes use of boost::python::extract<T>(val) to get a double value out of the argument. In general, the syntax is cleaner and more direct than using PyArg_ParseTuple. The remainder of the function calls Perform and retrieves the Results. As in the previous case of DescriptiveStatistics and LinearRegression, these are converted to a boost::python::dict and returned to the caller.

The Conversion Layer

As we have seen earlier, for the built-in types (bool, int, double, and so on) we can use one of the templated extract functions:

boost::python::extract<T>(val).

For conversion to the STL types, we have three inline'd functions. The first is a template function to_std_vector. This converts from a boost::python::object representing a list to a std::vector<T>. Listing 8-4 shows the code.

Listing 8-4. Converting a boost::python::object list to a std::vector

```
Conversion.h  ₽  ✕
StatsPythonBoost              ▾  {} Conversion                        ▾  ⊕ to_std_vector<T>(const boost::python::object & list)
    5            // Convert a Python list to a std::vector<T>
    6            template< typename T >
    7            inline std::vector< T > to_std_vector(const boost::python::object& list)
    8            {
    9                std::vector<T> results;
   10                for (boost::python::ssize_t i = 0; i < boost::python::len(list); ++i)
   11                    results.push_back(boost::python::extract<T>(list[i]));
   12                return results;
   13            }
```

Listing 8-4 starts by constructing an empty std::vector. Then, we iterate over the input list extracting the individual values and inserting them into the vector. We use this basic approach to illustrate accessing list elements in a standard manner. We could have used the boost::python::stl_input_iterator<T> to construct the results vector<T> directly from iterators. We use this function to convert a list of doubles to a vector of doubles and also to convert a list of string keys to a vector of strings.

The second function is `to_dict`. This is a specialized function used for converting the results set into a Python dictionary. Listing 8-5 shows the code.

Listing 8-5. Converting the results package to a Python dictionary

```
Conversion.h  -o  X
StatsPythonBoost              () Conversion              to_dict(const std::unordered_map<std::string,double>& _results, boost::python::dict & results)
    13         // Convert results set to a Python dictionary
    14         inline void to_dict(const std::unordered_map<std::string, double>& _results, boost::python::dict& results)
    15         {
    16             for (const auto& result : _results)
    17             {
    18                 results[result.first] = result.second;
    19             }
    20         }
    21
    22         // Convert data to a Python list
    23         inline void to_list(const std::vector<double>& data, boost::python::list& results)
    24         {
    25             for (const auto& d : data)
    26             {
    27                 results.append(d);
    28             }
    29         }
```

In this case, we input a `const` reference to a `std::unordered_map<std::string, double>` and return the contents into a `boost::python::dict` by simply iterating over the results. The final function is `to_list`. This is similar to the previous `to_dict` function. In this case, we create a Python `list` and populate it from a vector of `doubles`.

The Module Definition

Our Boost.Python module is defined in *module.cpp*. The module definition comprises both the functions and the classes that we want to expose to Python. We will deal with each in turn. The listing is quite long so has been broken up into two sections. First, Listing 8-6a shows the code that exposes the functions.

Listing 8-6a. The functions: StatsPythonBoost module definition

```
module.cpp  ⊣ ×
🔧 StatsPythonBoost            ▾    (Global Scope)                     ▾
      8        // Generate two function overloads for this function
      9        BOOST_PYTHON_FUNCTION_OVERLOADS(f_overloads, API::DescriptiveStatistics, 1, 2)
     10
     11  ⊟ BOOST_PYTHON_MODULE(StatsPythonBoost)
     12    {
     13        using namespace boost::python;
     14
     15        // Declare the functions that we are wrapping
     16  ⊟     def("DescriptiveStatistics", API::DescriptiveStatistics, f_overloads(args("data", "keys"),
     17            "Retrieve a package of descriptive statistics for the input data."));
     18        def("LinearRegression", API::LinearRegression,
     19            "Perform simple univariate linear regression: y ~ x, (where y = B0 + xB1).");
     20        def("SummaryDataTTest", API::StatisticalTests::SummaryDataTTest,
     21            "Summary data: population mean, sample mean, sample standard deviation, sample size.");
     22        def("OneSampleTTest", API::StatisticalTests::OneSampleTTest,
     23            "One-sample: population mean, sample.");
     24        def("TwoSampleTTest", API::StatisticalTests::TwoSampleTTest,
     25            "Two-sample: the underlying boost implementation assumes equal variances.");
     26
     27  ⊟     // Declare the TTest class
     28  ⊞     ...
     37
     38        // Declare the DataManager class
     39  ⊞     ...
     52    }
```

In Listing 8-6a, this part of the module definition should look somewhat familiar. It is not very different from the "raw" approach we saw in the previous chapter. We use the boost::python::def function to declare the functions we are wrapping. The first parameter is the function name we want to call from Python. The second parameter is the function address. The final parameter is the docstring. As pointed out earlier for the DescriptiveStatistics function, we want to be able to call it from Python with and without keys, and have it behave as the following interactive session demonstrates:

```
>>> import StatsPythonBoost as Stats
>>> data = [0, 1, 2, 3, 4, 5, 6, 7, 8, 9]
>>> results = Stats.DescriptiveStatistics(data)
>>> print(results)
{'Mean': 4.5, 'Count': 10.0, 'Kurtosis': -1.2000000000000002, 'Skew.P':
0.0, ... }
>>> keys = ['Mean', 'StdDev.P']
>>> results = Stats.DescriptiveStatistics(data, keys)
>>> print(results)
{'Mean': 4.5, 'StdDev.P': 2.8722813232690143}
```

In order to do this, we need two separate overloaded functions. This is the same approach that we used in the C++/CLI wrapper in Chapter 3. In this case, however, we do not need to explicitly write the overloads. We make use of the macro BOOST_PYTHON_ FUNCTION_OVERLOADS to generate the overloads for us. The arguments are the generator name, the function we want to overload, the minimum number of parameters (1 in this case), and the maximum number of parameters (2 in this case). Having defined this, we then pass the f_overloads structure, along with the docstring, to the def function.

The second part of the module definition, shown in Listing 8-6b, declares the classes that can be used directly in Python.

Listing 8-6b. The classes: StatsPythonBoost module definition

```
module.cpp ⊕ ×
StatsPythonBoost              ▼    (Global Scope)              ▼
10
11    ⊟BOOST_PYTHON_MODULE(StatsPythonBoost)
12    {
13          using namespace boost::python;
14
15          // Declare the functions that we are wrapping
16    ⊞ ...
26
27    ⊟    // Declare the TTest class
28    ⊟    class_<API::StatisticalTests::StudentTTest>("TTest",
29              init<const object&, const object&, const object&, const object&>(
30                  "Summary data: population mean, sample mean, sample standard deviation, sample size."))
31              .def(init<const object&, const list&>("One - sample: population mean, sample."))
32              .def(init<const list&, const list&>(
33                  "Two-sample: the underlying boost implementation assumes equal variances."))
34              .def("Perform", &API::StatisticalTests::StudentTTest::Perform, "Perform the t-test.")
35              .def("Results", &API::StatisticalTests::StudentTTest::Results, "Retrieve the results.")
36              ;
37
38          // Declare the DataManager class
39    ⊟    class_<API::Data::DataManager>("DataManager",
40              init<>("Default constructor."))
41              .def("CountDataSets", &API::Data::DataManager::CountDataSets,
42                  "Retrieve the number of data sets currently available.")
43              .def("Add", &API::Data::DataManager::Add,
44                  "Add the named data set to the collection.")
45              .def("GetDataSet", &API::Data::DataManager::GetDataSet,
46                  "Retrieve the named data set from the collection.")
47              .def("ListDataSets", &API::Data::DataManager::ListDataSets,
48                  "Retrieve the names of the data sets in the current collection.")
49              .def("ClearDataSets", &API::Data::DataManager::ClearDataSets,
50                  "Clear the data sets in the collection.")
51              ;
52    }
```

Listing 8-6b shows the `TTest` and `DataManager` classes that we wrap in this module. With these classes defined, we can write the following from a Python script, for example:

```
# Perform t-test from summary data
t: Stats.TTest = Stats.TTest(5, 9.261460, 0.2278881e-01, 195)
t.Perform()
print(t.Results())
```

The C++ wrapper class for the t-test is defined in *StatisticalTests.h*. The class template argument references our wrapper class. In this case, we have named it `StudentTTest` to distinguish it from the underlying `Stats::TTest` class. This class holds an instance of the underlying `Stats::TTest` class. The constructors determine the type of t-test to be performed and convert between `boost::python` types and the underlying C++ types, using the same conversions that we have seen.

From the module definition in Listing 8-6b, we can see that the first parameter is the name of the class, `"TTest"`. This is the name for the type we will call from Python. Alongside this, we define an `init` function (the constructor) which takes four arguments. We then define two additional `init` functions, one each for the remaining constructors with their corresponding arguments. Finally, we define the two functions `Perform` and `Results`. All the functions provide a `docstring`. That is all we need to do to expose a native C++ type to Python.

The `DataManager` class is exposed in a similar way. The C++ wrapper class is defined in *DataManager.h* in the namespace `API::Data`. This allows us to keep the wrapper class separate from the StatsLib C++ class of the same name. As before, the purpose of the wrapper class is to handle the type conversions and manage the lifetime of the underlying `DataManager` class in the StatsLib. Listing 8-7 shows a typical example function.

Listing 8-7. The `DataManager::ListDataSets` function

```
DataManager.cpp  ⊕ ×
[⬚] StatsPythonBoost          ▾ → API::Data::DataManager          ▾ | ⊕ ListDataSets() const
    43                 //
    44      ⊟         boost::python::list DataManager::ListDataSets() const
    45                 {
    46                     std::vector<Stats::DataSetInfo> datasets = m_manager.ListDataSets();
    47                     boost::python::list results;
    48
    49      ⊟             for (std::size_t i = 0; i < datasets.size(); ++i)
    50                     {
    51                         // Dataset name and count of elements
    52                         const auto& dataset = datasets.at(i);
    53                         results.append(boost::python::make_tuple(dataset.first, dataset.second));
    54                     }
    55                     return results;
    56                 }
```

From Listing 8-7 we can see that the function `ListDataSets` returns a Python `list` using the Boost.Python type. The list comprises `Stats::DataSetInfo` items that are typed as

```
using DataSetInfo = std::pair<std::string, std::size_t>;
```

The items contain the dataset name and the number of observations in the data. The function first obtains the currently loaded datasets from the `m_manager` member that this class wraps. Inside the for-loop, we use the function `boost::python::make_tuple` to create a Python `tuple` element with the dataset information. This is then appended to the results list and returned to the caller. The remaining functions are similarly straightforward.

Exception Handling

As in the previous chapter, exceptions should be handled and processed from the wrapper functions. In particular, we are concerned with bad arguments, so we should check types and report exceptions appropriately. We could use the same approach that we used in the previous chapter (manually translating C++ exceptions to Python exceptions). However, we can also take advantage of Boost.Python. In the module definition, the Boost.Python framework wraps our functions in the call to `.def(...)` so they are not called directly via Python. Instead, Python calls `function_call(...)` (*boost_1_76_0**libs**python**src**object**function.cpp*). This function wraps the actual function call in an exception handler. The exception handler handles the exception in the way that we did previously (*\boost_1_76_0\libs\python\src\errors.cpp*), though it catches and translates more exception types. This means Python does not halt and the exception is handled gracefully. We can test this out using the following Python code which passes in a string inside a list instead of the expected numeric item:

```
try:
    x = [1, 3, 5, 'f', 7]
    summary: dict = Stats.DescriptiveStatistics(x)
    print(summary)
except Exception as inst:
    report_exception(inst)
```

The error that is reported is

```
<class 'TypeError'>
No registered converter was able to produce a C++ rvalue of type double
from this Python object of type str
```

This error is provided by Boost. On the other hand, if we pass in an empty dataset, we get the following:

```
try:
    x = []
    summary: dict = Stats.DescriptiveStatistics(x)
    print(summary)
except Exception as inst:
    report_exception(inst)
```

The error that is reported is

```
<class 'ValueError'> The data is empty.
```

This is the error that is thrown from the underlying StatsLib. Basically, the same error handling that we wrote in the previous chapter is now provided for free.

PyBind

In this section, we develop our third and final Python extension module. This time we use PyBind. Boost.Python has been around for a long time and the Boost library that it is a part of offers a wide range of functionality. This makes it a relatively heavyweight solution if all we want to do is create Python extension modules. PyBind is a lighter-weight alternative. It is a header-only library that provides an extensive range of functions to facilitate writing C++ extension modules for Python. PyBind is available from here: `https://github.com/pybind/pybind11`.

Prerequisites

The only prerequisite for this section is to install PyBind into your Python environment. You can use either `pip install pybind` from a command prompt. Or you can download the wheel (`https://pypi.org/project/pybind11/#files`) and run `pip install "pybind11-2.7.0-py2.py3-none-any.whl"`.

Project Settings

The StatsPythonPyBind project is setup in a similar way to the previous one. It is a standard Windows DLL project. The project settings are summarized in Table 8-2.

Table 8-2. *Project settings for StatsPythonPyBind*

Tab	Property	Value
General	C++ Language Standard	ISO C++17 Standard (/std:c++17)
C/C++ > General	Additional Include Directories	*<Users\user>\Anaconda3\include* *<Users>\AppData\Roaming\Python\ Python37\site-packages\pybind11\include* *$(SolutionDir)Common\include*
Linker > General	Additional Library Directories	*<Users\user>\Anaconda3\libs* *$(BOOST_ROOT)\stage\lib*
Build Events > Post-Build Event	Command Line	(see in the following)

We create a module as before, copied to the script directory and renamed *.pyd*. We use the following script:

```
del "$(SolutionDir)StatsPython\$(TargetName).pyd"
copy /Y "$(OutDir)$(TargetName)$(TargetExt)" "$(SolutionDir)StatsPython\
$(TargetName)$(TargetExt)"
```

Additionally, we have removed the *pch* file and set the project setting to not using precompiled headers. Finally, we have added a reference to the StatsLib project in the project References. At this point, everything should build without warnings or errors.

Code Organization: module.cpp

In this project, there is only a single file, *module.cpp*. This file contains all the code. As we have seen in the previous section on Boost.Python and in the previous chapter as well, we have generally separated the conversion layer from the wrapped functions and classes. And we have separated these from the module definition. This was a convenient way to organize the code in the wrapper layer and allowed us to separate concerns (like converting types or calling functions) appropriately. However, PyBind simplifies both these aspects.

At the top of the file *module.cpp* we include the PyBind headers:

```
#include <pybind11/pybind11.h>
#include <pybind11/stl.h>
```

This is followed by our StatsLib includes.

Previously, we have had to declare wrapper/proxy functions that take Python types as arguments (either PyObject or boost::python::object) and convert these to the underlying native C++ types. With PyBind, we don't need to do this. We now have a single macro PYBIND11_MODULE that defines the module. The listing is quite long so we have divided it into three sections. The first section deals with the functions that we expose and the next two sections with the classes that we expose. The functions that we expose are shown in Listing 8-8a.

Listing 8-8a. The function definitions in the StatsPythonPyBind module

```
module.cpp  ⊣ ×
StatsPythonPyBind      ▼    (Global Scope)              ▼
  69      // Module definition
  70    ⊟PYBIND11_MODULE(StatsPythonPyBind, m)
  71     {
  72         m.def(
  73             "DescriptiveStatistics",
  74             &Stats::GetDescriptiveStatistics, py::arg("data"), py::arg("keys") = std::vector<std::string>(),
  75             R"pbdoc(Retrieve a package of descriptive statistics for the input data.)pbdoc"
  76         )
  77         .def(
  78             "LinearRegression",
  79             &Stats::LinearRegression,
  80             R"pbdoc(Perform simple univariate linear regression: y ~ x, (where y = B0 + xB1).)pbdoc"
  81         )
  82         .def(
  83             "SummaryDataTTest",
  84             &SummaryDataTTest,
  85             R"pbdoc(No-sample: TTest from summary data.)pbdoc"
  86         )
  87         .def(
  88             "OneSampleTTest",
  89             &OneSampleTTest,
  90             R"pbdoc(One-sample: single unknown population mean m; the population standard deviation s is unknown.)pbdoc"
  91         )
  92         .def(
  93             "TwoSampleTTest",
  94             &TwoSampleTTest,
  95             R"pbdoc(Two-sample: the underlying boost implementation assumes equal variances.)pbdoc"
  96         )
  97    ⊞...
 113         ;
 114         // This is the underlying TTest class; no wrapper required
 115    ⊞...
 131         // This is the underlying DataManager class; no wrapper required
 132    ⊞...
 144
 145    ⊞...
 150     }
```

The PYBIND11_MODULE macro defines the module name *StatsPythonPyBind* that is used by Python in the import statement. Inside the module definition, we can see the declarations of the DescriptiveStatistics and LinearRegression functions. The .def(...) function is used to define an exported function. Just as before, we give it a name that is called from Python and the final parameter which is a docstring.

However, unlike previously, we do not require a separate wrapper function. We can simply provide the underlying function address. This is the second parameter. The translation of both the parameters and the return type is handled by the PyBind framework. In the case of the Stats::GetDescriptiveStatistics function, which has a second default argument, we can provide further information about the argument structure. Specifically, PyBind allows us to specify the arguments and the default values if required, so we add the arguments after the function address, py::arg("data") and py::arg("keys") defaulted with the required value. Following this, the three functions SummaryDataTTest, OneSampleTTest, and TwoSampleTTest are now completely unnecessary. We have provided wrappers for illustration only. The code for the two-sample t-test wrapper is as follows:

```
std::unordered_map<std::string, double> TwoSampleTTest(const
std::vector<double>& x1, const std::vector<double>& x2)
{
    Stats::TTest test(x1, x2);
    test.Perform();

    return test.Results();
}
```

What is important here is not how the function wraps the TTest class, but rather the fact that the wrapper function uses native C++ and STL types both for the function parameters and the return value. Using Boost.Python, we would have had to convert from/to boost::python::object. But here we no longer need to convert from Python types to C++ types. Of course, we can, if we wish, explicitly wrap functions. This is a design choice.

The second part of the module definition deals with the class definitions. The TTest class is shown in Listing 8-8b.

Listing 8-8b. The description of the `TTest` class exported to Python

```
module.cpp  ⊕ ✕
StatsPythonPyBind         ▼   (Global Scope)              ▼  PYBIND11_MODULE(StatsPythonPyBind, m)
    69         // Module definition
    70     ⊟ PYBIND11_MODULE(StatsPythonPyBind, m)
    71     | {
    72     ⊞ ...
   114     |
   115     ⊟ ...
   120     |
   121     |        py::class_<Stats::TTest>(m, "TTest")
   122     |            .def(py::init<double, double, double, double>(),
   123     |                "Summary data: population mean, sample mean, sample standard deviation, sample size.")
   124     |            .def(py::init<double, const std::vector<double>& >(), "One-sample: population mean, sample.")
   125     |            .def(py::init<const std::vector<double>&, const std::vector<double>& >(),
   126     |                "Two-sample: the underlying boost implementation assumes equal variances.")
   127     |            .def("Perform", &Stats::TTest::Perform, "Perform the t-test.")
   128     |            .def("Results", &Stats::TTest::Results, "Retrieve the results.")
   129     |            .def("__repr__",
   130     ⊟              [](const Stats::TTest& a) {
   131     |                  return "<example.TTest>";
   132     |              }
   133     |        );
   134     |
   135     ⊞ ...
   152     |
   153     ⊞ ...
   158     | }
```

Listing 8-8b shows how the `TTest` class from the underlying C++ StatsLib is exposed to Python. As in the case of Boost.Python, we describe the type "TTest" that we want to use. But, in this case, the template argument to the `py::class_` object is the underlying `Stats::TTest` class. The class that is referenced is not a wrapper class, as was the case with Boost.Python. After the template arguments and the parameters passed to the constructor of `py::class_`, we use the `.def` function to describe the structure of the class. In this case, we declare the three `TTest` constructors with their respective arguments passed as template parameters to the `py::init<>` function. Again, it is worth highlighting that we do not need to do any conversions; we simply pass in native C++ types and STL types (rather than `boost::python::object` types). Finally, we declare the functions `Perform` and `Results`, and an anonymous function to return a string representation of the object to Python.

The definition of the `DataManager` class is equally straightforward. Listing 8-8c shows the class definition.

Listing 8-8c. The DataManager class definition

```
module.cpp  ⊐ ✕
StatsPythonPyBind          ▾   (Global Scope)                    ▾  ⊕ PYBIND11_MODULE(StatsPythonPyBind, m)
  69        // Module definition
  70     ⊟ PYBIND11_MODULE(StatsPythonPyBind, m)
  71      │ {
  72      ⊞ │...│
 114      │
 115      ⊞ │...│
 120      │
 121      ⊞ │...│
 134      │
 135     ⊟ │   // This is the underlying DataManager class; no wrapper required
 136     ⊟ │     py::class_<Stats::DataManager>(m, "DataManager")
 137      │         .def(py::init<>(), "Default constructor.")
 138      │         .def("CountDataSets", &Stats::DataManager::CountDataSets,
 139      │             "Retrieve the number of data sets currently available.")
 140      │         .def("Add", &Stats::DataManager::Add, "Add the named data set to the collection.")
 141      │         .def("GetDataSet", &Stats::DataManager::GetDataSet,
 142      │             "Retrieve the named data set from the collection.")
 143      │         .def("ListDataSets", &Stats::DataManager::ListDataSets,
 144      │             "Retrieve the names of the data sets in the current collection.")
 145      │         .def("ClearDataSets", &Stats::DataManager::ClearDataSets,
 146      │             "Clear the data sets in the collection.")
 147      │         .def("__repr__",
 148     ⊟ │             [](const Stats::DataManager& a) {
 149      │                 return "<DataManager> containing: " + to_string(a);
 150      │             }
 151      │         );
 152      │
 153      ⊞ │...│
 158      │ }
```

As we can see from Listing 8-8c, all we need to do in the .def function is to provide a mapping from the function names used by Python to the underlying C++ functions. Apart from the functions that are available in the DataManager class, we also have access to functions that form part of the definition of the Python class. For example, the DataManager extends the __repr__ function with a custom to_string function that outputs internal information regarding the dataset.

As we can see in this project, both the wrapper and the "conversion" layer are minimal. PyBind provides a wide range of facilities, allowing us to easily connect C++ code to Python. In this chapter, we have only just scratched the surface. There are a large number of features and we have only covered a fraction of them. Moreover, we are aware that we have really only written code for the most "vanilla" situations (taking advantage of the fact that PyBind allows us to do this easily).

However, while using PyBind makes exposing C++ classes and functions straightforward, we need to be aware that there is a lot going on under the hood. In particular, we need to be aware of the return value policies that can be passed to the `module_::def()` and the `class_::def()` functions. These annotations allow us to tune the memory management for functions that return a non-trivial type. In this project, we have only used the default policy `return_value_policy::automatic`. A full discussion of this topic is beyond the scope of this chapter. But, as the documentation points out, return value policies are tricky, and it's important to get them right.[1]

If we take a step back for a moment, we can see that in terms of the module definition, both Boost.Python and PyBind provide us with a meta-language for defining Python entities. It might seem a complicated way to go. Arguably, writing equivalent classes in native Python is somewhat easier than using a meta-language to describe C++ classes. However, the approach we have adopted here, describing native C++ classes, clearly addresses a different issue, that is, it provides a (relatively) easy way to export classes out of C++ and have them managed in an expected way in a Python environment.

Apart from defining the functions and classes, we have also been careful to add documentation strings. This is useful, and we can see this information if we print out the help on the class. This is shown in Listing 8-9 for the StatsPythonPyBind module.

---

[1] Chapter 7 Functions in the PyBind documentation (`https://pybind11.readthedocs.io/_/downloads/en/latest/pdf/`) provides full details.

Listing 8-9. Output from the Python `help` function for the `TTest` class

```
TERMINAL     PROBLEMS     OUTPUT     DEBUG CONSOLE
────────
>>> help(Stats.TTest)
Help on class TTest in module StatsPythonPyBind:

class TTest(pybind11_builtins.pybind11_object)
 |  Method resolution order:
 |      TTest
 |      pybind11_builtins.pybind11_object
 |      builtins.object
 |  Methods defined here:
 |
 |  Perform(...)
 |      Perform(self: StatsPythonPyBind.TTest) -> bool
 |
 |      Perform the t-test.
 |
 |  Results(...)
 |      Results(self: StatsPythonPyBind.TTest) -> Dict[str, float]
 |
 |      Retrieve the results.
 |
 |  __init__(...)
 |      __init__(*args, **kwargs)
 |      Overloaded function.
 |
 |      1. __init__(self: StatsPythonPyBind.TTest, arg0: float, arg1: float, arg2: float, arg3: float) -> None
 |
 |      Summary data: population mean, sample mean, sample standard deviation, sample size.
 |
 |      2. __init__(self: StatsPythonPyBind.TTest, arg0: float, arg1: List[float]) -> None
 |
 |      One-sample: population mean, sample.
 |
 |      3. __init__(self: StatsPythonPyBind.TTest, arg0: List[float], arg1: List[float]) -> None
 |
 |      Two-sample: the underlying boost implementation assumes equal variances.
 |
 |  __repr__(...)
 |      __repr__(self: StatsPythonPyBind.TTest) -> str
 |
 |  ----------------------------------------------------------------
 |  Static methods inherited from pybind11_builtins.pybind11_object:
 |
 |  __new__(*args, **kwargs) from pybind11_builtins.pybind11_type
 |      Create and return a new object.  See help(type) for accurate signature.
 |
```

Listing 8-9 shows the output from the StatsPythonPyBind module using the built-in `help()` function. We can see that it provides a description of the class methods and the class initialization along with the `docstrings` that we provided. It also provides detailed information both about the argument types used and the return types. We can see quite clearly how the declarative C++ class description has been translated into a Python entity. The output from StatsPythonBoost is similar, though not identical, and worthwhile comparing. As an alternative to the help function, we can use the `inspect` module to introspect on our Python extension. The `inspect` module provides additional useful functions to help get information about objects. This can be useful if you need to display a detailed traceback. As expected, we can retrieve all the information from our module except, of course, the source code. What both these approaches serve to illustrate is that, with a limited amount of C++ code, we have developed a proper Python object.

Exception Handling

As expected, the PyBind framework provides support for exception handling. C++ exceptions, `std::exception` and its subclasses, are translated into the corresponding Python exceptions and can be handled in a script or by the Python runtime. Using the first of the two examples that we used previously, the exception report from Python is as follows:

```
<class 'TypeError'>
DescriptiveStatistics(): incompatible function arguments. The following
argument types are supported:
    1. (arg0: List[float]) -> Dict[str, float] Invoked with: [1, 3,
    5, 'f', 7]
```

The exception handling provides sufficient information to determine the cause of the issue and processing can proceed appropriately. It is worth pointing out that PyBind's exception handling capabilities go beyond simple translation of C++ exceptions. PyBind provides support for several specific Python exceptions. It also supports registering custom exception handlers. The details are covered in the PyBind documentation.

The Python "Client"

Now that we have built a working PyBind module, it would be good to try out some of the functionality. We could of course have created a full-featured Python application. But we prefer to keep things simple and focused. As on previous occasions, we are concerned not just with exercising the underlying functionality, but also with interoperating with other Python components. Unlike in previous chapters, we have not written dedicated unit tests using one of the (several) Python testing frameworks. Instead, we use a simple Python script *StatsPython.py* that extends the basic script which we used in the previous chapter. We use the alias `Stats` as a simple expedient:

```
import StatsPythonPyBind as Stats
#import StatsPythonBoost as Stats
```

This allows us to easily switch between the Boost.Python extension module and the PyBind extension module. This is not proposed as a general approach, it just facilitates testing the functions and classes here.

The script itself defines functions that exercise the underlying StatsLib functionality. It also allows us to do a simple side-by-side test of the TTest class, for example. Listing 8-10 shows the function run_statistical_tests2.

Listing 8-10. A simple function to compare the results from two t-tests

```
80    def run_statistical_tests2(df_x1: pd.DataFrame, df_x2: pd.DataFrame) -> None:
81        """ Run more statistical tests """
82        try:
83            x1: list = df_x1.iloc[:, 0].tolist()
84            x2: list = df_x2.iloc[:, 0].tolist()
85
86            results: dict = Stats.TwoSampleTTest(x1, x2)
87            print(results)
88
89            t: Stats.TTest = Stats.TTest(x1, x2)
90            t.Perform()
91            print(t.Results())
92        except Exception as inst:
93            report_exception(inst)
94
```

In Listing 8-10, the function takes as inputs two Pandas data frame objects (simple datasets loaded from *csv* files) and converts them to lists, the type our Python interface to StatsLib expects. The first call uses the procedural interface. The second identical call constructs an instance of the TTest class that we declared and calls the functions Perform and Results. Both approaches produce the same results, unsurprisingly.

Performance

One of the reasons for trying to connect C++ and Python is the potential for performance gains from C++ code. To this end, we have written a small script, *PerformanceTest.py*. We want to test the performance of the mean and (sample) standard deviation functions. We would like to do this for Python vs. PyBind computing Mean and StdDev for 500k items.

From the Python side we have two approaches. Firstly, we define the functions `mean`, `variance`, and `stddev`. The implementations of these only use basic Python functionality. We also define the same functions, this time using the Python statistics library. This allows us to have two different baselines.

From the C++ side, we make a minor adjustment to the PyBind module definition so that we can expose the functions `Mean` and `StandardDeviation` from the StatsLib. In the case of the `Mean` function, this is quite straightforward to do. The functions exist in the `Stats::DescriptiveStatistics` namespace and are defined in the static library. Using the PyBind wrapper, StatsPythonPyBind, all we need to do is to add the description shown in Listing 8-11 to the module definition.

Listing 8-11. Enhancing the module definition with additional C++ functions

```
module.cpp    ⊟ ✕
StatsPythonPyBind          ▾   (Global Scope)              ▾   ⊘ PYBIND11_MODULE(StatsPythonPyBind, m)
    97    ⊟      .def(
    98                "Mean",
    99                &Stats::DescriptiveStatistics::Mean,
    100               R"pbdoc(Compute the mean of the data.)pbdoc"
    101           )
```

In Listing 8-11, we add the function `"Mean"`, supply the address of the C++ implementation, and add the documentation string.

The `StandardDeviation` function is slightly more involved. The underlying C++ function takes two parameters, a `std::vector<double>` and an enumeration for the `VarianceType`. If we just pass the function address to the module definition, we will get a runtime error from Python as the function expects two arguments. To address this, we need to extend the code. At this point we have a choice. We can either write a small wrapper function that provides a hardcoded `VarianceType` argument or we can expose the `VarianceType` enumeration. We'll look at both approaches.

First off, we look at writing a small wrapper function. Listing 8-12 shows this approach.

Listing 8-12. Wrapper for the underlying `StandardDeviation` function

```
module.cpp  ⊕  ✕
StatsPythonPyBind        ▼    (Global Scope)              ▼  ● SampleStandardDeviation(const std::vector<double>& data)
  39
  40    ⊟ double SampleStandardDeviation(const std::vector<double>& data)
  41      {
  42          using namespace Stats::DescriptiveStatistics;
  43          return StandardDeviation(data, VarianceType::Sample);
  44      }
```

Wrapping a function with a hardcoded argument is not exactly ideal, but it is simple. In the module definition, we add the following declaration shown in Listing 8-13.

Listing 8-13. Definition of the `SampleStandardDeviation` wrapper function

```
module.cpp  ⊕  ✕
StatsPythonPyBind        ▼    (Global Scope)              ▼  ● SampleStandardDeviation(const std::vector<double>& data)
  106           ).def(
  107               "StdDevS",
  108               &SampleStandardDeviation,
  109               R"pbdoc(Compute the standard deviation of the data.)pbdoc"
  110           )
```

In Listing 8-13, we use the name "StdDevS" to reflect the fact that we are requesting the sample standard deviation. Now we can use this function in our performance test.

An alternative to writing the wrapper function is to expose the `VarianceType` enumeration to Python. If we do this, then we could call the function as follows:

```
>>> data = [0, 1, 2, 3, 4, 5, 6, 7, 8, 9]
>>> Stats.StdDev(data, Stats.VarianceType.Sample)
3.0276503540974917
>>> Stats.StdDev(data, Stats.VarianceType.Population)
2.8722813232690143
```

To accomplish this in the code, we need to make two small changes. First, we describe the enumeration in the module. This is shown in Listing 8-14.

Listing 8-14. Defining the enumeration for `VarianceType`

```
module.cpp    ⊕  ✕
StatsPythonPyBind              ▼   (Global Scope)                    ▼  ⊕ PYBIND11_MODULE(StatsPythonPyBind, m)
    112
    113           py::enum_<Stats::DescriptiveStatistics::VarianceType>(m, "VarianceType")
    114               .value("Sample", Stats::DescriptiveStatistics::VarianceType::Sample)
    115               .value("Population", Stats::DescriptiveStatistics::VarianceType::Population)
    116               ;
```

In Listing 8-14, we use the PyBind `py::enum_` class to define the enumeration `VarianceType` and give it a name. Notice that we have "attached" the enum to the module context (the `m` parameter in the `py::enum_` function) in this case as it is not part of a class, for example. We then add appropriate strings for the corresponding values. A more detailed description of `py::enum_` is given in the PyBind documentation. We also need to make a small modification to the way the function is defined in the module to reflect the fact that it is expecting two parameters. This is shown in Listing 8-15.

Listing 8-15. Defining additional arguments for the `StdDev` function

```
module.cpp    ⊕  ✕
StatsPythonPyBind              ▼   (Global Scope)                    ▼  ⊕ PYBIND11_MODULE(StatsPythonPyBind, m)
    102           .def(
    103               "StdDev",
    104               &Stats::DescriptiveStatistics::StandardDeviation,
    105               py::arg("data"), py::arg("VarianceType"),
    106               R"pbdoc(Compute the standard deviation of the data.)pbdoc"
    107           )
```

In Listing 8-15, we have added two `py::arg` structures to the function definition. This is similar to the way in which we handled the second optional argument for the `GetDescriptiveStatistics` function. The code compiles without warnings or errors. We can test that it works as expected using the Python interactive shell, as follows:

```
>>> Stats.VarianceType.__members__
{'Sample': <VarianceType.Sample: 0>, 'Population': <VarianceType.
Population: 1>}
```

With these modifications in place, we can return to the performance test. The *PerformanceTest.py* script is straightforward. We import the required libraries, including StatsPythonPyBind. We define two versions of both `mean` and `stddev` in Python. One version doesn't use the statistics library and the second version does. This just facilitates the comparison between Python functions and our library functions. We add a simple test function that uses random data and returns the `mean` and `stddev` with timing information.

These are the results we obtain (running the pure Python functions, rather than the Python statistics library which we might reasonably expect to perform faster):

```
Running benchmarks with COUNT = 500000
[mean(x)] (Python implementation) took 0.005 seconds
[stdev(x)] (Python implementation) took 3.003 seconds
[Mean(x)] (C++ implementation) took 0.182 seconds
[StdDevS(x)] (C++ implementation) took 0.183 seconds
```

The Python function `mean(x)` is about two orders of magnitude faster than the native C++ function. Changing the C++ code to use a `for-loop` instead of `std::accumulate` made no significant difference. It might be interesting to investigate if the latency in the C++ side is due to the conversion layer or simply unnecessary copying of vectors. Nevertheless, the native C++ `StdDev` function is substantially faster than either of the Python variants.

The Statistics Service

In the StatsPython project, there is a script *StatsService.py* that launches a small Flask app. The Flask app is a simple demonstration of a web service. It is extremely limited and only allows the user to compute a summary data t-test. The main page is shown in Figure 8-1.

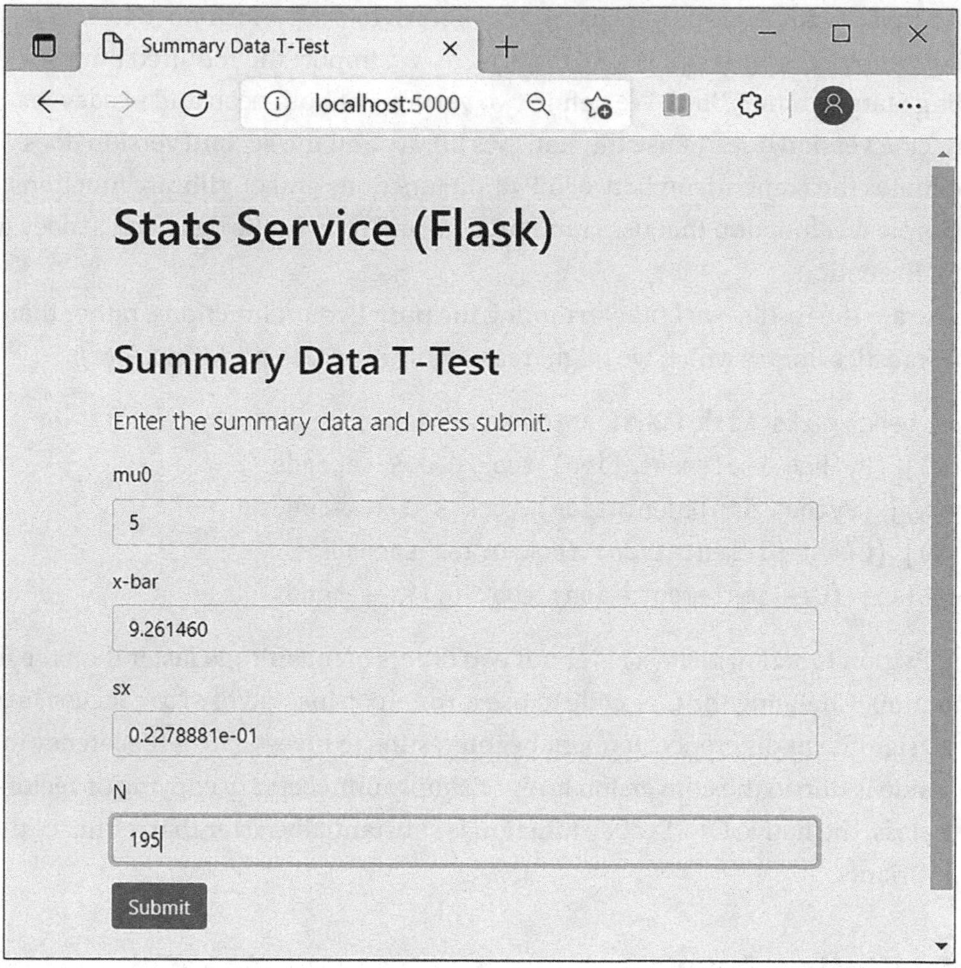

Figure 8-1. *The Stats Service main page*

The main page consists of a simple form that allows the user to input the parameters of a summary data t-test. After pressing the *Submit* button, we compute the required values and return them, as shown in Figure 8-2.

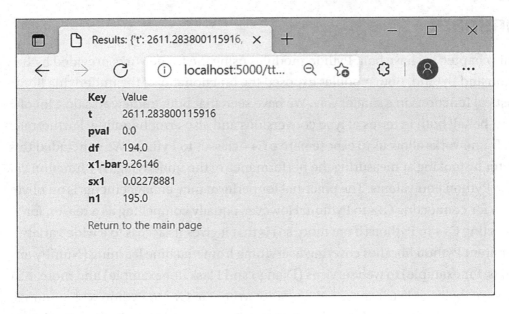

Figure 8-2. *Results from a summary data t-test*

To run the service, open the StatsPython project in VSCode, for example. From the terminal, type

```
> py .\StatsService.py
```

This starts the Flask service on port 5000. In your browser address bar, go to *http://localhost:5000/*. This points to the Summary Data T-Test page which is the main page for this app. Fill in the required details and press submit. The results are returned as expected, using the underlying TTest class from the StatsPythonPyBind module.

Apart from the small amount of code required to get this up and running, what is worth emphasizing is what we have achieved in terms of a multi-language development infrastructure. We have got an infrastructure that allows us to develop and adapt native C++ code, build this into a library, incorporate the library into a Python module, and have this functionality available for use in a Python web service. This flexibility is valuable when developing software systems.

Summary

In this chapter, we have built Python modules using the frameworks provided by Boost. Python and PyBind. Both modules exposed the functionality of the underlying library of statistical functions in a similar way. We have seen that both frameworks do a lot of work on our behalf both in terms of type conversions and also error handling. Furthermore, both frameworks allow us to expose native C++ classes to Python. We concluded this chapter by looking at measuring the performance of the underlying C++ function calls vs. the Python equivalents. The potential for performance enhancements is an obvious reason for connecting C++ to Python. However, equally compelling as a reason for connecting C++ to Python (if not more so) is that it gives us access to a wide variety of different Python libraries covering everything from machine learning (NumPy and Pandas, for example) to web services (Django and Flask, for example) and more. As we have seen, being able to expose functionality written in C++ to Python with minimal effort gives you a useful additional architectural choice when developing loosely coupled software systems.

Additional Resources

The links that follow provide more in-depth coverage of the topics dealt with in this chapter.

- The main reference for Boost.Python is the excellent Boost documentation `www.boost.org/doc/libs/1_77_0/libs/python/doc/html/index.html` and the reference manual at `www.boost.org/doc/libs/1_77_0/libs/python/doc/html/reference/index.html`. There is also a useful tutorial covering exposing classes: `www.boost.org/doc/libs/1_77_0/libs/python/doc/html/tutorial/tutorial/exposing.html`.

- The excellent PyBind documentation at `https://pybind11.readthedocs.io/en/latest/` has a lot of useful information.

Exercises

The exercises in this section deal with exposing the same functionality as previously, but this time via the Boost.Python module and the PyBind module.

The following exercises use the StatsPythonBoost project:

1)   In StatsPythonBoost, add procedural wrappers for the z-test functions. These should be almost identical to the t-test functions. No additional conversion functions are required.

- In *StatisticalTests.h,* add these declarations for the three functions:

```
boost::python::dict SummaryDataZTest(const
boost::python::object& mu0, const boost::python::object&
mean, const boost::python::object& sd, const
boost::python::object& n);

boost::python::dict OneSampleZTest(const
boost::python::object& mu0, const boost::python::list& x1);

boost::python::dict TwoSampleZTest(const
boost::python::list& x1, const boost::python::list& x2);
```

- In *StatisticalTests.cpp,* add the implementations of these functions. Follow the code for the t-test wrapper functions.

- In *module.cpp,* add the three new functions to the module `BOOST_PYTHON_MODULE(StatsPythonBoost) {}`

- After rebuilding StatsPythonBoost, open the StatsPython project in VSCode. Open the *StatsPython.py* script. Add functions to test the z-test functions using the data we have used previously. For example, we can add the following function:

```python
def one_sample_ztest() -> None:
    """ Perform a one-sample z-test """
    try:
        data: list = [3, 7, 11, 0, 7, 0, 4, 5, 6, 2]
        results = Stats.OneSampleZTest(3.0, data)
        print_results(results, "One-sample z-test.")
    except Exception as inst:
        report_exception(inst)
```

2) In the StatsPythonBoost project, add a `MovingAverage` function.

- In *Functions.h* add the following declaration:

```cpp
boost::python::list MovingAverage(const boost::python::list&
dates, const boost::python::list& observations,
const boost::python::object& window);
```

- In *Functions.cpp*:

  - Add `#include "TimeSeries.h"` to the top of the file.

  - Add the implementation: the function takes three non-optional arguments: a list of dates, a list of observations, and a window size.

  - Convert the inputs using the existing conversion functions and pass these to the constructor of the `TimeSeries` class.

  - Return the results using the `Conversion::to_list` function.

- In *module.cpp*, add the new function:

```cpp
def("MovingAverage", API::MovingAverage, "Compute a simple
moving average of size = window.");
```

- Build StatsPythonBoost. It should build without warnings and errors. You should be able to test the MovingAverage function interactively, adapting the script we used previously.

- Open the StatsPython project in VSCode. Open the *StatsPython.py* script. Add a function to test the moving average, including exception handling. Run the script, and debug if required.

3)   In the StatsPythonBoost project, add a TimeSeries class that wraps the native C++ TimeSeries class and computes a simple moving average.

The steps required are as follows:

- Add a *TimeSeries.h* and a *TimeSeries.cpp* file to the project. These will contain the wrapper class definition and implementation, respectively.

- In *TimeSeries.h*, add the class declaration. For example:

```
namespace API
{
    namespace TS
    {
        // TimeSeries wrapper class
        class TimeSeries final
        {
        public:
// Constructor, destructor, assignment operator and
MovingAverage function

        private:
            Stats::TimeSeries m_ts;
        };
    }
}
```

- In *TimeSeries.cpp,* add the class implementation. The constructor converts the `boost::python::list` arguments to appropriate `std::vector` types. The `MovingAverage` function extracts the window size argument and forwards the call to the `m_ts` member. The results are returned using the `Conversion::to_list()` function.

- In *module.cpp*, add the include file, and add the class declaration to `BOOST_PYTHON_MODULE(StatsPythonBoost)` as follows:

```
// Declare the TimeSeries class
class_<API::TS::TimeSeries>("TimeSeries",
init<const list&, const list&>("Construct a time series from
a vector of dates and observations."))
.def("MovingAverage", &API::TS::TimeSeries::MovingAverage,
        "Compute a simple moving average of size = window.")
    ;
```

- After rebuilding StatsPythonBoost, open the StatsPython project in VSCode. Open the *StatsPython.py* script. Add a function to test the moving average, including exception handling. Run the script, debug if required.

The following exercises use the StatsPythonPyBind project:

4) Add procedural wrappers for the z-test functions. These should be almost identical to the t-test functions. No additional conversion functions are required.

- In *module.cpp*, add declarations/definitions for the three functions.

- In the module definition, add entries for these three functions. Follow the code for the t-test wrapper functions.

- After rebuilding the StatsPythonPyBind project, open the StatsPython project in VSCode. Open the *StatsPython.py* script. Add functions to test the z-test functions using the data we have used previously.

5)   Add a new class ZTest to PYBIND11_MODULE. Follow the definition of the TTest class, for example:

```
py::class_<Stats::ZTest>(m, "ZTest")
    .def(py::init<double, double, double, double>(), "...")
    .def(py::init<double, const std::vector<double>& >(),
    "...")
    .def(py::init<const std::vector<double>&, const
    std::vector<double>& >(), "...")
    .def("Perform", &Stats::ZTest::Perform, "...")
    .def("Results", &Stats::ZTest::Results, "...")
    .def("__repr__", [](const Stats::ZTest& a) {
                return "<example.ZTest>";
            }
);
```

Note that in this case, no separate wrapper is required. We can simply reference the underlying native C++ class.

- After rebuilding the StatsPythonPyBind project, open the StatsPython project in VSCode. Open the *StatsPython.py* script. Add functions to test the z-test functions using the data we have used previously. We can extend the function we used previously to test the one-sample z-test to test both the procedural wrapper and the class as follows:

```
def one_sample_ztest() -> None:
    """ Perform a one-sample z-test """
    try:
        data: list = [3, 7, 11, 0, 7, 0, 4, 5, 6, 2]
        results = Stats.OneSampleZTest(3.0, data)
        print_results(results, "One-sample z-test.")

        z: Stats.ZTest = Stats.ZTest(3.0, data)
        z.Perform()
        print_results(z.Results(), "One-sample z-test.
        (class)")

    except Exception as inst:
        report_exception(inst)
```

The results output from both calls should be identical.

6)   In the StatsPythonPyBind project, add a `MovingAverage` function.

- In *module.cpp,* add #include "TimeSeries.h".

- In *module.cpp,* add a declaration/definition of the wrapper function.

```
std::vector<double> MovingAverage(const std::vector<long>&
dates, const std::vector<double>& observations, int window)
{
        Stats::TimeSeries ts(dates, observations);
        const auto results = ts.MovingAverage(window);
        return results;
}
```

- In *module.cpp,* add the definition of the `MovingAverage` function to the list of functions exposed by the `PYBIND11_MODULE`.

- After rebuilding the StatsPythonPyBind project, open the StatsPython project in VSCode. Open the *StatsPython.py* script. Add a function to test the moving average, including exception handling. Run the script, debug if required.

7)   Expose the native C++ `TimeSeries` class and the simple moving average function.

- In *module.cpp,* add the include file, and add the class declaration. The class definition will be similar to the class definition we added to the StatsPythonBoost project previously.

```
py::class_<Stats::TimeSeries>(m, "TimeSeries")
    .def(py::init<const std::vector<long>&, const
    std::vector<double>&>(),
        "Construct a time series from a vector of dates and
        observations.")
    .def("MovingAverage", &Stats::TimeSeries::MovingAverage,
    "Compute a simple moving average of size = window.")
```

```
    .def("__repr__",
        [](const Stats::TimeSeries& a) {
            return "<TimeSeries> containing: " +
            to_string(a);
        }
);
```

To properly add the __repr__ method, we would need to adapt the underlying class definition to allow access to the internals or write an additional to_string() method. This is left as a further final exercise.

- After rebuilding the StatsPythonPyBind project, open the StatsPython project in VSCode. Open the *StatsPython.py* script. Add a function to test the moving average, including exception handling. Run the script, debug if required.

It is worth emphasizing that exposing the ZTest class and the TimeSeries class using PyBind has been quite straightforward, compared to the amount of work required to expose wrappers either via CPython or the Boost.Python wrapper.

CHAPTER 9

Conclusion

Our goal in this book has been to develop components that connect a C++ codebase (albeit a simple, slightly artificial one) to client software written in other languages, specifically C#, R, and Python. The intention has been to make the functionality in a C++ library available and to allow access to this functionality from other client languages. This is what we have accomplished. In doing so, we have covered quite a lot of ground.

We started off by building a C++ library of statistical functions. This has formed the basis of what we want to expose to clients. The reasoning was that it was simple enough to understand but more complete than a toy example. It has enough features to illustrate real-world issues when developing wrapper components that connect to other languages. Throughout the book, we have let the source code drive what we want to expose, and while this has limited the coverage somewhat, it is also more manageable.

On top of this C++ codebase, we have built wrapper components that allow us to expose the C++ functionality to different languages. Firstly, we built a C++/CLI assembly. We saw just how easy it was to use in a number of different contexts. We exercised the functionality in a simple console client – testing both the functions we call and how the component interoperates with other C# libraries (in this case Accord.NET). We also connected our component to Excel via Excel-DNA with minimal effort.

After this, we built an R package that uses Rcpp to connect the C++ codebase to R. As before, we exercised the basic functionality, but also had a look at using the StatsR component with other R packages, in particular `tidyverse`, `ggplot`, and `benchmark`. Finally, we built a small Shiny App as a demonstration of how our component interacts with other R packages. We saw how the StatsR package can be used anywhere in the extensive R universe. In the process, we set up a development infrastructure that consists of an IDE (CodeBlocks) for building C++ code using the compiler required by R, and an IDE for writing Rcpp packages (RStudio), which we can use to develop and build the packages.

© Adam Gladstone 2022
A. Gladstone, *C++ Software Interoperability for Windows Programmers*,
https://doi.org/10.1007/978-1-4842-7966-3_9

Lastly, we have also built Python extension modules: three to be exact. We saw the potential pitfalls of using the low-level CPython approach and then looked at using both Boost.Python and PyBind as frameworks to connect C++ to Python. We saw how both frameworks facilitate development of wrapper components. We also saw that potential performance gains (not guaranteed) were only one of a number of possible reasons for connecting C++ to Python. Bringing a new component into the Python universe to operate seamlessly alongside libraries like NumPy and Pandas is also significant.

Overall, we have looked at how to set up projects for the different language wrapper components. We have spent some time looking at the design of the wrappers: the separation of concerns into a functional layer, the part making the call, and the type conversion layer. We have looked at details of type conversions and also how they might be usefully generalized. Along the way, we touched upon a number of other software development topics: some code-related, like exception handling; others related to the development process like testing and debugging. Beyond simply building components, we have set up a tooling infrastructure that eases the (multi-language) development process.

On the other hand, in restricting ourselves to exposing the underlying functionality in a limited C++ library, there are a number of important areas we have ignored. We haven't touched on threading and concurrency in a native C++ library and how this could be exposed to different client languages. From the perspective of the actual components, there are various areas that we have omitted. In C#, we haven't covered delegates; in R, we haven't covered extending the modules; and in Python, we have barely scratched the surface of using PyBind. All these could require a book to themselves. What we have offered here are a number of starting points for future development.

At a more general level, the intention has been to extend the architectural choices available when developing software. In Chapter 2, we saw some of the limitations of housing a component directly in a Windows application (linking to the component *lib* or *dll*). We have demonstrated that a viable alternative is to develop wrapper components (assemblies, packages, and modules) that can be used in multiple contexts (Windows applications, web applications) and from different languages, C#, R, and Python. This leads to a more loosely coupled software system. The components themselves can offer quite heterogeneous services, but they interoperate because they participate in the underlying framework, whether it is .NET via C++/CLI, R via Rcpp, or Python.

Boost Libraries

Introduction

At various points in this book, we need to use the Boost libraries. Specifically, we have two aspects that we need and which are prerequisites for some of the projects. The first is that we use the Boost.Math libraries for some of the basic statistics and also for performing the t-test. Specifically, we use the cdf of the Student's t-distribution to compute the p-value (`https://en.wikipedia.org/wiki/Student%27s_t-distribution`). The second requirement is that we need a built version of the Boost. Python libraries. This build needs to be consistent with the version of Python that we are targeting in order to build the Python extension modules. In this case, we use Python version 3.8.

This appendix provides a brief guide to installing and building the Boost libraries, specifically addressing the two aspects highlighted earlier. There are several different ways to do this, and this is just one.

The following link provides more detailed instructions if needed: `www.boost.org/doc/libs/1_76_0/more/getting_started/windows.html`.

Installation

1. Download the Boost libraries and unpack it to install a complete Boost distribution.

    The root directory will be *\boost_1_76_0*...

2. Set the system environment variable `BOOST_ROOT` to the corresponding root directory of the boost installation.

213

© Adam Gladstone 2022
A. Gladstone, *C++ Software Interoperability for Windows Programmers*,
https://doi.org/10.1007/978-1-4842-7966-3

Building

3. We need to build Boost.Python, and so we first need to configure the Boost build.

Open the file *\boost_1_76_0\tools\build\src\user-config.jam*

Add the following line:

```
using python : 3.8 ;
```

and save the changes.

Open the command prompt and change your current directory to the Boost root directory. Then, type the following command:

```
bootstrap
```

The first command prepares the Boost.Build system for use.

Then type `.\b2`

The second command invokes Boost.Build to build the separately compiled Boost libraries. Then be patient, as indicated by the Boost.Build system.

Finally, check that the libraries have been built. Specifically, you need the following:

- *\boost_1_76_0\stage\lib\libboost_python38-vc142-mt-gd-x32-1_76.lib*

- *\boost_1_76_0\stage\lib\libboost_python38-vc142-mt-x32-1_76.lib*

- *\boost_1_76_0\stage\lib\libboost_python38-vc142-mt-gd-x64-1_76.lib*

- *\boost_1_76_0\stage\lib\libboost_python38-vc142-mt-x64-1_76.lib*

In reality, we do not use the 32 bit libraries in this project; however, it is worth having them available should you want to target Win32.

References

The two main references are

```
www.boost.org/doc/libs/1_76_0/more/getting_started/windows.html
```
and
```
www.boost.org/doc/libs/1_76_0/libs/python/doc/html/building.html
```

CMAKE

Introduction

This appendix describes the StatsLibCM project. This is a CMake project to build a static library (*libStatsLibCM.a*) using the MinGW GCC toolset (the same toolset installed by CodeBlocks). The project output (*libStatsLibCM.a*) should be exactly the same as the outputs produced by building the Debug and Release builds, respectively, with CodeBlocks. The only difference in this project is that we specify everything using *CMakeLists.txt*.

The advantage of this project is that it can be opened in Visual Studio Community Edition 2019. And the targets can be built from there. Hence, this project could be added to the solution file *SoftwareInteroperability.sln*, and could substitute usage of CodeBlocks when building the ABI-compatible version of the statistics library for R.

Project Setup

There are two main files in the *\StatsLibCM* project directory. *CMakeSettings.json* contains the project settings. *CMakeLists.txt* contains the CMake instructions for building the project. Open *CMakeSettings.json* (double-click on the file). Figure B-1 shows the main view.

© Adam Gladstone 2022
A. Gladstone, *C++ Software Interoperability for Windows Programmers*,
https://doi.org/10.1007/978-1-4842-7966-3

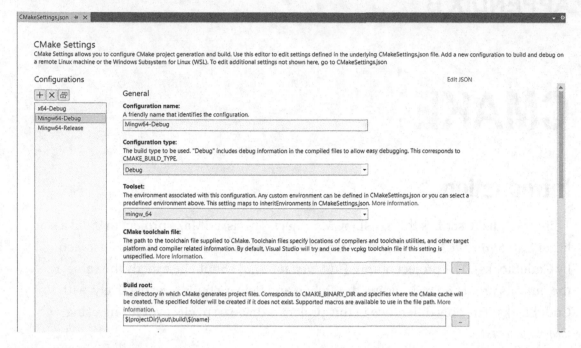

Figure B-1. *CMake Settings*

On the left-hand side, we can see the Configurations. There are currently three configurations. The x64-Debug configuration is the Windows default. We have added two further configurations: MinGW64-Debug and MinGW64-Release. When the configurations are added, depending on how your environment is set up, the paths may or may not be correct. The Visual Studio default settings for the MinGW toolset were different from my environment. To correct this requires editing the *CMakeSettings.json*. Under "Mingw64-Debug", "environments", we have added the following block:

```
{
  "MINGW64_ROOT": "D:/Program Files/mingw-w64/x86_64-8.1.0-posix-seh-rt_v6-
  rev0/mingw64",
  "BIN_ROOT": "${env.MINGW64_ROOT}/bin",
  "FLAVOR": "x86_64-w64-mingw32",
  "TOOLSET_VERSION": "8.1.0",
  "PATH":
  "${env.MINGW64_ROOT}/bin;${env.MINGW64_ROOT}/../usr/local/bin;${env.
  MINGW64_ROOT}/../usr/bin;${env.MINGW64_ROOT}/../bin;${env.PATH}",
```

```
  "INCLUDE":
"${env.INCLUDE};${env.MINGW64_ROOT}/include/c++/${env.TOOLSET_
VERSION};${env.MINGW64_ROOT}/include/c++/${env.TOOLSET_VERSION}/tr1;${env.
MINGW64_ROOT}/include/c++/${env.TOOLSET_VERSION}/${env.FLAVOR}",
  "environment": "mingw_64"
}
```

And we have added the same under release. This configures the path to the GCC toolset.

The *CMakeLists.txt* file contains the CMake configuration. There are a large number of options. The variables are described in the CMake documentation here: `https://cmake.org/cmake/help/latest/manual/cmake-variables.7.html`.

Building the Outputs

Once the project is opened, select the configuration you want to build and Build All. The targets are output in subdirectories of the StatsLibCM project. You can check that the build output functions correctly in R by editing *Makevars.win* under the StatsR project, in *\src*. Change the line #PKG_LIBS to point to the debug or the release build of the library:

#PKG_LIBS="<your path>/SoftwareInteroperability/StatsLibCM/out/build/ Mingw64-Debug/**libStatsLibCM.a**

Following this, do a Clean and Rebuild in RStudio and run the tests.

References

Duffy, D.J. & Germani, A. (2013). C# for Financial Markets. John Wiley & Sons, Chichester.

Eddelbuettel D. (2013). Seamless R and C++ Integration with Rcpp. Use R! Springer, New York.

Fletcher, S. & Gardner, C. (2009). Financial Modeling in Python. John Wiley & Sons, Chichester.

Fraser, Stephen R.G. (2009). Pro Visual C++/CLI and the .Net 3.5 Platform. Apress.

Heege, Marcus (2007). Expert Visual C++/CLI .Net for Visual C++ Programmers. Apress.

Kabacoff, Robert. (2015). R in Action. Manning Publications, New York.

Lott, Steven F. (2016). Modern Python Cookbook. Packt Publishing.

Nelli, Fabio. (2018). Python Data Analytics. Apress.

Ragunathan, Vivek (2016). C++/CLI Primer: For .Net Development. Apress.

Wickham, Hadley & Grolemund, Garrett. (2017). R for Data Science. O'Reilly Media, Inc.

Wilkes, Matthew (2020). Advanced Python Development. Apress.

© Adam Gladstone 2022
A. Gladstone, *C++ Software Interoperability for Windows Programmers*,
https://doi.org/10.1007/978-1-4842-7966-3

Index

A

Accord.NET, 67, 68, 70, 72, 85, 211
Application
    Console, 7, 8, 10, 18, 26, 31, 33, 34, 36,
        67, 68, 85
    MFC, 31, 33, 165
    Windows GUI, 34
    Windows WPF, 34, 73
Application Binary Interface, 8, 91
Architecture
    choices, 41, 45, 202, 212
    loosely coupled, 202
Arrange-act-assert pattern, 27, 54
Assembly
    private, 73
    shared, 73

B

Boost
    BOOST_PYTHON_FUNCTION_
        OVERLOADS macro, 182
    BOOST_ROOT, 25, 175, 213
    installation, 213
    version, 3

C

C#, 8–10, 34, 46, 54, 67–88, 140, 211
C++
    classes, 23, 46, 126, 128, 129, 173,
        192, 202

codebase, 4, 11, 30, 35, 111, 211
C++17 Standard, 25, 43, 149, 175, 186
    high-performance, 131, 195–197, 199
    object oriented, 58, 91, 126, 154
    statistical functions, 41, 91, 102, 110,
        173, 211
    structured bindings, 14
C++/CLI, 7, 41–66, 68, 76, 88, 211
CMake, StatsLibCM, 93, 215
CmdLet, 77
CodeBlocks
    installation, 92, 93
    version, 93
Common Language Runtime (CLR)
    support, 43, 44
Compiler
    GCC, 91–93, 110, 111
    GCC, 91
    gcc toolchain, 92, 102
    MSVC, 91
Components
    assembly, 73, 85
    bridging layer, 34
    extension modules, 162
    library, 8, 9, 11
    package, 23
    wrapper, 4, 8, 10, 37, 45, 62, 67, 110,
        135, 149, 173, 211, 212
COM wrapper, 33, 61, 62
Correlation coefficient, 36, 64, 138
CPython, 7, 52, 148, 167, 168, 212
Cross-platform development, 4, 93

221

Printed in the United States
by Baker & Taylor Publisher Services